The Staircase to Heaven

A Biblical Journey from Mormonism to Grace

To my husband, Mark, without whom I would have never started this journey.

Table of Contents

The Rules of this Book 10
Articles of Faith 13
Early Church History 16
The Mormon Word 28
The Absence of Evidence 35
Church Hierarchy 48
The Nature of God 58
Grace & Original Sin 66
Revelations & Prophecy 81
Salvation 92
Zion 106
The Not-So-Mormon Word 109
The Christianity Debate 125
Baptism, Sacraments & the Holy Spirit 130
Restatements, Revised Explanations & Contradictions 144
Law & Church 175
Mormon Missionaries 180
Marriage & Polygamy 185
Moralism 195
Blacks in the Church 206
Trial by Church 209
Tithing & Finances 215
Being Prepared, Providing for the Poor 218
Mormon Temples 222
Coming to Terms with Grace 227

Preface

Church was three hours. It was always three hours, starting with Sacrament, then going to joint classes, and then going to girl's classes. I would sit impatiently through Sacrament, drawing on the program and leaning over to put my head on my mother's lap so she would play with my hair. It was the first Sunday of the month, typically reserved for the bearing of testimonies. One by one, brave churchgoers would walk up to the pulpit and start with, "I'd like to bear my testimony that I know this church is true…"

I was born in Orem, Utah and grew up in the Mormon Church, also called the Church of Jesus Christ of Latter Day Saints. My parents, my grandparents, my entire family is Mormon on both sides and has been since the pioneers walked across the plains and settled in Utah. My parents were married in the Salt Lake City temple and I was baptized into the Mormon Church at the age of eight. It wasn't until I was about sixteen that I left the church, about the same age as many people who exchange going to church for sleeping in.

From childhood, I was always an incredibly independent person. Of course, the teenage years always magnify this independence, when we are trying to jump into adulthood as quickly as possible. I was strong-willed, as most sixteen year olds are. I thought I knew best, and thought I knew exactly what I wanted in life. But Mormonism wasn't just a religion, it was a lifestyle. Constantly being judged if I even thought about drinking a cup of coffee or accidently used the word 'crap' or wore a one-piece swimsuit but didn't wear a shirt over it. I didn't want to sit in class and learn how to sew or do crafts.

I wasn't only capable of being a housewife or a mother – I wanted more than that. I wanted to learn how to be a successful adult with a good job, and contribute my gifts to the world. Beyond that, my friends who were Baptists, Methodists, Catholics and the like were all telling me that my religion wasn't even Christian. How could I possibly listen to those accusations without taking a step back from my faith?

By the time I was seventeen, I had become an inactive member in the church. I didn't belong to any religion, although Mormonism was all I had ever known. In fact, I didn't even know where to start. All I knew was what I had been told, and nothing more. Words like grace, trinity and communion were foreign concepts; words that existed in modern day Christianity but had nothing to do with my faith.

When I was eighteen I went to college, where I met my now-husband. He grew up in a Christian school with a Lutheran background. His family was strong in their faith and it was important to him that we were too, and so we began attending a Lutheran Church near the University together on Sundays.

A little after we began attending this church, I called the Pastor to schedule a meeting with him. He sat down with me and listened while I explained that I grew up Mormon, but I had no idea what I believed anymore. Like a sheep reunited with its flock, the Pastor began to guide me back into faith. Of course, Mormonism is very different from most Christian religions so the Pastor had to really do his homework. He began doing research on Mormonism in an effort to better explain Christianity to me, and I began realizing how much I didn't even know about the religion I came from.

How is it possible to attend a church every Sunday for sixteen years and still have no idea about what you believe? I realized at that point that I had spent so much time worrying about living up to a lifestyle of perfection and good works, I had neglected the religious aspects altogether.

I went through confirmation classes and became re-baptized into the Lutheran Church. My husband and I have a home church now in Houston, Texas with a truly magnificent Pastor. Upon transferring our membership, we became members of their CORE class, where we revisited all of the basics of our faith. It was in our first class that I got the idea for this book.

Some people may be questioning why I would choose to write such a book. Why write a book dedicated to a religion to which you no longer belong? Why explain the beliefs of an entire group of people when you do not share those beliefs? Growing up I knew that I was unsure about what I had been taught. I looked around at all other religions and wondered why they were considered 'normal' while mine could cause such controversy and outrage. People would ask me if we thought a spaceship was coming to take us away, or if I had four moms, or if I had twenty brothers and sisters.

I wrote this book for several reasons. Mormonism is one of the most misunderstood and misinterpreted religions on the planet. There are more religious Christian zealots who pass judgment on this group of people than any other, and it is mostly because Mormons consider themselves to be Christian.

Countless times I have gotten into religious debates with Christians who believe what they believe, but don't understand how to interpret their beliefs to a person of the LDS faith. Instead, they attack the Mormon beliefs without adequately explaining their own and how they differ.

As I started my research of the Mormon doctrine and their beliefs in an effort to further my own understanding of Christianity, I was surprised by how difficult it was to find a non-judgmental, facts-only type of literature on the subject. I don't want to know 'how to witness to Mormons' or 'things you should tell Mormons' from the perspective of a person who has never been an insider.

For all intensive purposes, I was still Mormon in my mind because I wasn't yet dedicated in my heart to anything else. Most people were either so enraged on the subject that they were condemning people of the faith to hell, or they were Mormons themselves who loved their lifestyle and that was the only vantage point they could offer.

If you have never really been a Mormon – going to church with them, defending yourself from your Christian friends at school, waking up at five in the morning to go to Seminary and eating Sunday dinner with the Missionaries – then you just don't really know Mormonism.

It was my goal and my purpose in writing this book to gain a further understanding of my family and their beliefs, but doing so through their eyes and having physically been an 'insider' once myself. My goal was to take you on the same journey that I am taking now, starting this book as a Mormon and finishing it in grace.

As Christians, we know that we have a responsibility to spread the Word. While we stand in our Sanctuaries and speak to God and grow a relationship with God, Mormons are standing in their Sanctuary and speaking with their God and growing a relationship with their God as well.

These are not people who find God to be absent in their lives – these are people who are deeply convicted in their beliefs and have been, in many cases like myself, since childhood. How can you possibly reach out to an entire community of people without first understanding who they are, what they do, and why they believe the way they believe? You can't. And that is exactly why I have written this book.

The Rules of This Book

There are a few principles under which I operate in this book, and I would like to explain before we really start digging into the good stuff.

<u>Who this Book is for</u>

First, I will often refer to 'mainstream Christians'. For the purpose of this book, mainstream Christians will be defined as any religious groups who believe in the basic principles of Christianity as explained in the Nicene Creed:

"I believe in one God, the Father Almighty, maker of heaven and earth, and of all things visible and invisible. And in one Lord Jesus Christ, the only-begotten Son of God, begotten of His Father before all worlds, God of God, Light of Light, very God of very God, begotten, not made, being of one substance with the Father; by whom all things were made; who for us men and for our salvation came down from heaven, and was incarnate by the Holy Spirit of the virgin Mary and was made man; and was crucified also for us under Pontius Pilate. He suffered and was buried. And the third day He rose again according to the Scriptures and ascended into heaven and sits at the right hand of the Father. And He will come again with glory to judge both the living and the dead, whose kingdom will have no end. And I believe in the Holy Spirit, the Lord and giver of life, who proceeds from the Father and the Son, who with the Father and the Son together is worshiped and glorified, who spoke by the prophets. And I believe in one holy Christian and apostolic Church. I acknowledge one Baptism for the remission of sins, and I look for the resurrection of the dead and the life of the world to come. Amen."

I readily admit that not all Christian churches read and recite the Nicene Creed, nor do they always incorporate this creed into their religious practice. However, this is an ancient creed written to establish commonality between all people of Christian faith in the early establishment of the church, and all mainstream Christian churches should agree with the basic principles, story, and nature of God established by this creed. If your faith agrees with this creed, I consider you to be included in the 'mainstream Christianity' group mentioned throughout this book.

Differences Divide Us

Second, it is my goal to remain 'denomination-neutral' throughout this book. For that reason, I will not be diving too deep into sacrament, baptism, or rituals as it would be impossible for me to do an effective comparison on those topics without possessing a bias opinion. In an effort not to create denominational divisions, I will refrain from digging too deep into certain subjects that are controversial.

The point is to focus on the differences between Mormons and mainstream Christians, and not Mormons and Baptists, Catholics, Lutherans, Methodists, etc. Since Mormons do not fundamentally believe in principles of the Nicene Creed or the nature of God as mainstream Christians do, they are also not considered to be another denomination. They are simply 'Mormon', and I will elaborate on these differences throughout this book. I will focus only on those subjects that make up the foundation of Christianity, and what sets Mormons apart from mainstream Christians.

Plain as the Letters on the Page

Third, I will only be using scriptural references throughout this book, be they Mormon scriptures or the Bible accepted by mainstream Christians. All Mormon scriptures, journals or quotations will only come from Mormon-sanctioned sources. It is not my goal to provide information hosted by anti-Mormon sources. Instead, I will be providing Biblically-based arguments and only utilizing information that has been approved and is in circulation by the Mormon Church, at the time this book is being written.

Sorry, it's all in Old English

Fourth, throughout this book I will be citing the King James Version of the Bible. While this is a more difficult English Bible to read, it is the only version of the Bible approved for use in the Mormon Church. In an effort to speak apples-to-apples with Mormons using their own doctrine, I will only be utilizing this version of the Bible. However, if there is a verse referenced in this book that you are having difficulties understanding, I do suggest you review other Bible translations to help further your comprehension.

That's a Fact

Fifth, I will often state Mormon doctrine as fact. Simply because I am saying 'God said' or 'God revealed' does not imply that I actually believe in any way that God said or revealed those things. The things that God says or reveals in Mormon doctrine are factual within the confines of the Mormon Church, as that is what they believe.

There are two perspectives in this book, one from the view of Mormons and one from the view of mainstream Christians. I can speak on both sides of the fence by experience. My goal is to appeal to the logic of both parties, and explain the Mormon doctrine in such a way that it makes sense.

The Road Goes on Forever

Sixth, this book is my personal journey. When I started writing this book, I was Mormon. When I finished writing this book, I was Christian. I wanted to help people understand Mormons, and in doing so, I really ended up helping myself. The issues and discussion points that I have brought up in this book are from my own personal perspective on Mormonism versus Christianity. These are the issues I trudged through, the questions raised in my own mind, and my own conclusions. My logic may not help all people and you may disagree with me on points. That is your personal right! But if it helps just one person to walk this same journey and find grace, it's good enough for me.

ARTICLES OF FAITH

As a child, I can vividly remember discussing and memorizing the Articles of Faith. Over and over again, we would discuss these articles and their impact over our behavior. We would say them, memorize them, and sing them every single Sunday. We would put on little shows for our parents and discuss them constantly. As a child, they were just words. It was not until I was about twenty-five years old before I actually read those words, and looked at them in a deeper context than the songs we would sing on Sundays.

The Articles of Faith are not unlike the many creeds that exist in mainstream Christianity. They are simple statements of faith, and usually a starting point for youth in the Mormon Church. I recall the teachers having posters, visually illustrating to us the articles of faith while we recited them and memorized each one. I still sing those songs in my head when I read these articles.

Just like the Old Days

The articles of faith were created in the 1830's, upon the establishment of the Mormon Church, and is not unlike the many creeds found and widely accepted in mainstream Christianity. To provide a little history, the Nicene Creed (amongst other creeds in mainstream Christianity) was created shortly after the establishment of the first Christian church.

In 318 A.D., there began to be contentions between leaders of the Christian movement. All churches were independent of each other and Christian beliefs were not uniform amongst all Christians. Emperor Constantine called the Council of Nicaea in June of the year 325 A.D., in an effort to bring all church leaders together and formulate a common thread of understanding and belief between all churches.

There were 318 bishops believed to be in attendance. The goal of this council was not to create any new doctrine, but rather to define the beliefs of the Christian Church in hopes to create unity amongst all Christians. Collectively, the Nicene Council established what is known today as the Nicene Creed.

Just as the Nicene Creed was established hundreds of years ago, the Mormons created their own Articles of Faith to confirm and unify their faith. If you take a bit of time to read these articles, you will see that they bring to light some very fundamental differences between Mormons and mainstream Christians.

These differences span all the way from the nature of God, to the meaning of grace, to salvation itself. In understanding Mormonism, we have to understand these principles and how they are inherent to the Mormon faith – and how mainstream Christianity lines up relative to these beliefs.

The 13 Articles of Faith

1. We believe in God, the Eternal Father, and in His Son, Jesus Christ, and in the Holy Ghost.

2. We believe that men will be punished for their own sins, and not for Adam's transgression.

3. We believe that through the Atonement of Christ, all mankind may be saved, by obedience to the laws and ordinances of the Gospel.

4. We believe that the first principles and ordinances of the Gospel are: first, Faith in the Lord Jesus Christ; second, Repentance; third, Baptism by immersion for the remission of sins; fourth, laying on of hands for the gift of the Holy Ghost.

5. We believe that a man must be called of God, by prophecy, and by the laying on of hands by those who are in authority, to preach the Gospel and administer in the ordinances thereof.

6. We believe in the same organization that existed in the Primitive Church, namely, apostles, prophets, pastors, teachers, evangelists, and so forth.

7. We believe in the gift of tongues, prophecy, revelation, visions, healing, interpretation of tongues, and so forth.

8. We believe the Bible to be the word of God as far as it is translated correctly; we also believe the Book of Mormon to be the word of God.

9. We believe all that God has revealed, all that He does now reveal, and we believe that He will yet reveal many great and important things pertaining to the Kingdom of God.

10. We believe in the literal gathering of Israel and in the restoration of the Ten Tribes; that Zion (the New Jerusalem) will be built upon the American continent; that Christ will reign personally upon the earth; and, that the earth will be renewed and receive its paradisiacal glory.

11. We claim the privilege of worshiping Almighty God according to the dictates of our own conscience, and allow all men the same privilege, let them worship how, where, or what they may.

12. We believe in being subject to kings, presidents, rulers, and magistrates, in obeying, honoring, and sustaining the law.

13. We believe in being honest, true, chaste, benevolent, virtuous, and in doing good to all men; indeed, we may say that we follow the admonition of Paul—we believe all things, we hope all things, we have endured many things, and hope to be able to endure all things. If there is anything virtuous, lovely, or of good report or praiseworthy, we seek after these things.

Early Church History

Since the history of the Mormon Church is quite young (relative to the age of the Bible and modern Christianity), its history is paramount to understanding the fundamentals of the Mormon belief. Joseph Smith founded the church on his own revelations, visions and beliefs. This portion of the church's history is crucial to its development over time and its prominence today.

It is important to note that all of the information I will be providing in this chapter has been taken directly from the Mormon Doctrine, in this case primarily the Pearl of Great Price section entitled *The History of Joseph Smith* (which I will site hereafter as HJS). As I mentioned before, throughout this book the only Biblical references I will provide are from the King James Version of the Bible, as that is the only version of the Bible accepted within Mormonism.

From the Beginning

Joseph Smith was born on December 23, 1805. Born to Joseph Smith Senior and Lucy Mack Smith, he was the fifth of eleven children in their Christian home. Mormons believe that God Himself called upon Joseph Smith to be the latter day prophet and restore God's true gospel to the earth.

"I the Lord, knowing the calamity which should come upon the inhabitants of the earth, called upon my servant Joseph Smith and spake unto him from heaven, and gave him commandments" Doctrine & Covenants, 1:17. The LDS church says that over the several hundred years since Christ's death, the church had fallen into apostasy, or rejection of the original teachings of the Church. They maintain that the teachings of the Bible, through translations and transcriptions, had been corrupted and the original ordinances of salvation had been changed.

Joseph Smith, then age 14, prayed in the woods alone in an effort to know which church was true. He referenced James 1:5, reading "if any of you lack wisdom, let him ask of God, that giveth to all men liberally, and unbraideth not; and it shall be given him." It was in the spirit of this verse that he says he began to pray with God. Joseph Smith then stated in HJS 1:15, ". . . immediately I was seized upon by some power which entirely overcame me, and had such an astonishing influence over me as to bind my tongue so that I could not speak. Thick darkness gathered around me, and it seemed to me for a time as if I were doomed to sudden destruction." Joseph cried out to God to deliver him from his enemies, and with his cries appeared a light.

In HJS 1:17, he says "I saw two personages, whose brightness and glory defy all description, standing above me in the air. One of them spake unto me, calling me by name and said, pointing to the other – *this is my beloved Son. Hear him.*" In this portion of the Church History, it is clear that this is the revelation which spawned the direct rejection of the teachings of the Trinity. Instead, the Trinity was replaced here by worship of God and Jesus as two separate entities. They are seen and represented within Mormonism as two separate and distinct beings, not of one essence.

Joseph asked God and Jesus what church he should join, and "I was answered that I must join none of them, for they were all wrong" HJS 1:19. Joseph then went home and spoke with his mother about what he had seen. A few days later, Joseph spoke with a Methodist preacher who dismissed his vision of God, saying that his vision must have been from the devil because visions and revelations ceased to exist along with the Apostles. As a fourteen year old boy, very few people believed in his stories of visions and he quickly fell subject to persecution.

Joseph continued to maintain his belief that he had seen a vision, working at his vocation until September 21, 1823. At this time Joseph was praying by his bed when he saw a blinding light and then "a personage appeared at my bedside, standing in the air, for his feet did not touch the floor" HJS 1:30. This personage called Joseph by name saying "that he was a messenger sent from the presence of God to me, and that his name was Moroni; that God had work for me to do" History of the Church 1:33.

This is a key point in the Mormon Church history, because it was at this point that the Book of Mormon was introduced. Moroni (mə-rō'nī) continued to speak to Joseph, saying ". . . there was a book deposited, written upon gold plates, giving an account of the former inhabitants of this continent, and the source from whence they sprang. He also said that the fullness of the everlasting Gospel was contained in it, as delivered by the Savior to the ancient inhabitants" History of Joseph Smith 1:34. This is the first introduction of the golden plates, to be known as the Book of Mormon. A more in-depth look at this book and its contents is explained later in this book.

And then... Jesus went to America...

I find it interesting that the Mormons maintain that Jesus was in America when there is no mention of America in the Bible. In fact, after Jesus' resurrection, 1 Corinthians 15:4-9 says, "And that he was buried, and that he rose again the third day according to the scriptures: and that he was seen of Cephas, then of the twelve: after that, he was seen of above five hundred brethren at once; of whom the greater part remain unto this present, but some are fallen asleep. After that he was seen of James; then of all the apostles. And the last of all he was seen of me also, as of one born out of due time. For I am the least of the apostles, that am not meet to be called an apostle, because I persecuted the church of God." In fact, the Bible provides specific names and groups of people who did see Jesus after His resurrection. Yet not one time does the Bible say, 'and then he went to America'.

Moroni: Now you see him, now you don't

As a person of the Mormon faith at one point, I can attest to the fact that there are dozens of stories about how the Book of Mormon could have possibly been translated from an ancient language of native America. I have been told that there were magic glasses, angels and helpers sent to translate it. I have been told that we don't need to worry about how it was translated at all, and worrying about things like that shows a lack of faith. I have even been told that the Book of Mormon is stupid and that Mormons believe that aliens came to translate it.

To set the record straight, this is explained in History of Joseph Smith 1:35, ". . . there were two stones in silver bows – and these stones, fastened to a breastplate, constituted what is called the Urim and Thummim – deposited with the plates; and the possession and use of these stones were what constituted "seers" in ancient or former times; and that God had prepared them for the purpose of translating the book." At this moment, Joseph had not yet actually seen these plates or the seer stones, he had only heard of their existence from the Angel Moroni.

He says then that Moroni told him that he could not show Joseph the plates yet, but when he did Joseph could only show them to those people who God said were acceptable. If he showed them to people unworthy to see them, Joseph would be destroyed. Then Joseph says, "While he was conversing with me about the plates, the vision was opened to my mind that I could see the place where the plates were deposited" History of Joseph Smith 1:42. After this vision, the Angel Moroni disappears.

Just as soon as Moroni disappears, he reappears again and tells Joseph of the grievous things that would happen to the Earth in Jesus' coming. After this second, brief visit, he again ascended back to Heaven. Then Moroni appears again, and repeats over and over the same things that he had said before. He also added this time a caution, telling Joseph that Satan would try to tell him to sell the plates for money. Moroni tells Joseph that he must have no other intentions in his heart than to use the plates to glorify God, or he would not get to see them.

His discussions with Moroni lasted through the night. He rose the next morning without sleeping the night before, and began to proceed with his usual chores. His father saw his physical exhaustion throughout the morning and instructed him to go back home and rest. Travelling back to the house, Joseph collapsed and awoke again to the Angel Moroni speaking to him, again telling him the same things he had the night before.

Moroni then told Joseph to go and tell his father everything that he had said to him. Joseph did as he was told, telling his father everything that he saw in his vision. His father told him that this vision was from God, and he should do as he was instructed. He left his father and went to the field he was shown by Moroni in the vision the night before.

Joseph found the plates in a stone box, buried under a hill in Manchester, New York. In the stone box he found the golden plates, the Urim and Thummim, and the breastplate. In the bottom of the box were "two stones crossways of the box and on these stones lay the plates and other things with them. I made an attempt to take them out, but was forbidden by the messenger, and was again informed that the time for bringing them forth had not yet arrived, neither would it, until four years from that time; but he told me that I should come to that place precisely in one year from that time, and that he would there meet with me, and that I should continue to do so until the time should come for obtaining the plates." Joseph went to the hill at the end of each year, finding Moroni there each time. Moroni gave him instructions and education on what God was going to do and God's kingdom at each of their meetings.

Joseph & the Plates of Gold

On January 18, 1827, Joseph Smith married a young woman named Emma Hale. Knowing Joseph's history of divine visions, Emma's family disapproved of their marriage. Since he was persecuted by Emma's family, he moved with her to another city in New York. On September 22, 1827, Joseph went again to the hill and met with Moroni. This time, however, Moroni gave the plates to Joseph, telling him that he was responsible for them. He was instructed to keep them safe, or risk God taking them away.

At this point, Joseph asserts in his History of Joseph Smith 1:60 that "the most strenuous exertions were used to get them from me." The persecution worsened and people tried to steal the plates, but he continued to keep them safe. On May 2, 1838, Moroni visited again requesting that Joseph give the plates back and Joseph complied. "They remained safe in my hands, until I had accomplished by them what was required at my hand. According to arrangements, the messenger called for them, I delivered them up to him; and he has them in his charge until this day."

The Mormon Church maintains that the golden plates were taken up by Moroni into heaven, and that is why there is no physical evidence of these plates in existence today.

The persecution continued and became so severe that Joseph and his wife moved to Pennsylvania. Prior to their trip, they met a gentleman named Martin Harris, a farmer from New York, who offered Joseph fifty dollars to help him along his journey. With this money, Joseph and Emma moved to Pennsylvania where Joseph began translating the plates. He copied many characters off of the plates, and began translating them using the Urim and Thummim.

At this time, Martin Harris came to Joseph's home where he got the characters drawn off of the plates and took them back to New York with them. Harris took them to Charles Anthon, a professor of literary studies. In History of Joseph Smith 1:64, Harris is noted saying, "Professor Anthon stated that the translation was correct, more so than any he had before seen translated from the Egyptian. I then showed him those which were not yet translated, and he said that they were Egyptian, Chaldaic, Assyriac, and Arabic; and he said they were true characters. He gave me a certificate, certifying to the people of Palmyra that they were true characters, and that the translation of such of them as had been translated was also correct." Harris took the certificate and put it in his pocket.

On his way out the door, the professor called him back and asked how Joseph found the gold plates. Harris responded that an angel of God had revealed it to Joseph, and with that it is said that the professor tore the certificate to pieces, saying that if the plates were brought to him, he would translate them himself. Joseph refused to provide the professor with the plates, which is why Joseph says he could not attain the documentation stating that the translation is correct.

Joseph & his Best Buddy Oliver

On April 5, 1829, Joseph Smith met Oliver Cowdery for the first time. Oliver told Joseph that he taught in the neighborhood where his father lived and was boarded for a few months at his father's house. Joseph's family told Oliver about how Joseph received the plates, and Oliver went to Joseph to inquire about them. Two days after he arrived, Oliver began writing for Joseph as he translated the Book of Mormon.

Having read about baptism for the remission of sins in the plates, Joseph and Oliver went into the woods to pray and ask to be baptized. "While we were thus employed, praying and calling upon the Lord, a messenger from heaven descended in a cloud of light, and having laid his hands upon us, he ordained us, saying: Upon you my fellow servants, in the name of Messiah, I confer the Priesthood of Aaron, which holds the keys of the ministering of angels, and of the gospel of repentance, and of baptism by immersion for the remission of sins; and this shall never be taken again from the earth until the sons of Levi do offer again an offering unto the Lord in righteousness" History of Joseph Smith 1:68-69.

The messenger told Joseph that this Aaronic priesthood did not contain the power of laying on of hands for the gift of the Holy Ghost, but that they would have the opportunity to receive that power later. The messenger also told Oliver to baptize Joseph, and have Joseph baptize Oliver.

Joseph and Oliver then went to baptize each other and give each other the Aaronic Priesthood. This part of the church's history is very interesting, as this is the first place where the Book of Mormon uses Biblical references. In the History of Joseph Smith 1:72, Joseph says, "The messenger who visited us on this occasion and conferred this Priesthood upon us, said that his name was John, the same that is called John the Baptist in the New Testament, and that he acted under the direction Peter, James and John, who held the keys of the Priesthood of Melchizedek, which Priesthood, he said, would in due time be conferred on us, and that I should be called the first Elder of the Church, and he (Oliver Cowdery) the second. It was on the fifteenth day of May, 1829, that we were ordained under the hand of this messenger, and baptized."

It is here that Joseph is actually saying that John the Baptist himself actually came down from heaven to baptize Joseph and Oliver, and tell them of the Melchizedek priesthood. It is also saying that Peter, James and John also held the Melchizedek priesthood, and that John named Joseph the President of the church. The order of Melchizedek is referenced several times in the Bible, primarily in the book of Hebrews. The Mormons use the orders established in the Old Testament as the foundation of their organizational structure, which will be discussed later in this book.

Sorry, only one Revelator allowed

It was immediately following their baptisms that Joseph and Oliver begin to make prophesies of things that would happen in the future and the rise of the Mormon Church. They both decided to keep their Priesthood and Baptisms secret, to escape the prosecution that would surely ensue. Throughout the History of Joseph Smith, there are several references to scriptural secrets – things that Joseph could not and did not share with the common people of his church. For example, in 1:20 he says, "And many other things did he say unto me, which I cannot write at this time," and in 1:41 he says, "He quoted many other passages of scripture, and offered many explanations which cannot be mentioned here."

There came a time in the Mormon faith when, feeling inspired by the capacity of Joseph Smith to experience revelations, people in the Mormon Church began claiming that they too could experience revelations. However, Joseph Smith put these claims to rest when God spoke to him, saying, "But behold, verily, verily, I say unto thee, no one shall be appointed to receive commandments and revelations in this church excepting my servant Joseph Smith, for he receiveth them even as Moses" Doctrine & Covenants 28:2. Joseph Smith was the sole prophet of the Mormon Church. This principle is still in practice today, where the President of the Church is the only person capable of receiving these revelations.

In June of 1829, the translation of the Book of Mormon was finally complete. Nearly a year later, the first edition of the Book of Mormon was published and the Doctrine & Covenants – including the revelations of Joseph Smith – was accepted as Mormon doctrine as well. With the Book of Mormon in-hand, Joseph and his small group of followers set out to grow the Mormon Church. Over the next year, these church followers would begin to become organized.

Building a Name for Itself

Up to this point in the Mormon Church's history, the church did not have an official name. It was not until April 26, 1838 that Joseph received a revelation pertaining to how the church was to be named, "And also unto my faithful servants who are of the high council of my church in Zion, for thus it shall be called, and unto all the elders and people of my Church of Jesus Christ of Latter-day Saints, scattered abroad in all the world; For thus shall my church be called in the last days, even The Church of Jesus Christ of Latter-day Saints" Doctrine & Covenants 115:3-4. From that point forward they gained that long name, often referred to as the LDS church.

Also in this same revelation was the building of a temple, "therefore, I command you to build a house unto me, for the gathering together of my saints, that they may worship me" Doctrine & Covenants 115:8. They were instructed to labor until there was nothing left incomplete.

Within Joseph Smith's instructions were also another interesting instruction, "Verily I say unto you, let not my servant Joseph, neither my servant Sidney, neither my servant Hyrum, get in debt any more for the building of a house unto my name" Doctrine & Covenants 115:13. When I read that last verse, I had to ask myself why God would disallow Joseph's debt. God asked people to sacrifice much more than finances in the Bible – why would he not want Joseph to incur debt at the expense of building God's church? Interesting.

The Martyr of Mormons

A short few years later on June 27, 1844, Joseph Smith and his brother Hyram Smith were murdered while imprisoned in Carthage, Illinois. They were murdered by a mob of around 200 people, and revered later by the Mormon community as martyrs. In Doctrine & Covenants 135:3, it was said, "Joseph Smith, the Prophet and Seer of the Lord, has done more, save Jesus only, for the salvation of men in this world, than any other man that ever lived in it . . . and like most of the Lord's anointed in ancient times, has sealed his mission and his works with his own blood." Joseph Smith was only thirty-eight years old when he was murdered.

The Mormon Church maintains that Joseph Smith was placed in jail on false charges, saying, "They were innocent of any crime, as they had often been proved before, and were only confined in jail by the conspiracy of traitors and wicked men; and their innocent blood on the floor of Carthage jail is a broad seal affixed to 'Mormonism' that cannot be rejected by any court on earth" Doctrine & Covenants 135:7.

Within the Mormon faith, the President of the Church is the only person with the capabilities to receive revelations from God. Doctrine & Covenants 28:6-7, "And thou shalt not command him who is at thy head, and at the head of the church; for I have given him the keys of the mysteries, and the revelations which are sealed, until I shall appoint unto them another in his stead." Upon Joseph Smith's death, these powers were bestowed upon the next President of the Church.

Moving to the Valley

Following the death of Joseph Smith, the persecution of the Mormon Church had become quite severe, with some cities calling for an extermination order for all Mormons in the area. In response, the Mormons began to move west across America, being called pioneers in church history. In 1847, Brigham Young became the Second President of the Mormon Church, and he led the people to the Salt Lake City Valley. Brigham Young led the Mormon Church until 1877 when he passed away. One year later, the Brigham Young Academy – now well known by many as Brigham Young University – was established in Provo, Utah.

Growing up so Fast

In 1880, John Taylor became the President church. At that time, the Pearl of Great Price was also added into the Mormon cannon of scripture. He died just seven years later, leaving Wilford Woodruff to take the lead of the Mormon people. During Wilford Woodruff's presidency, it was revealed to him by God that the practice of plural marriage should be brought to an end. The ending of plural marriage is documented in the Doctrine & Covenants, Official Declaration One. The relationship between the

Mormon faith and polygamy will be addressed later in this book, as it contributes greatly to the views and steroetypes of the Mormon Church. Eight years after changing the church's view on polygamy, Wilford Woodruff passed away and left the Presidency to be resumed by Lorenzo Snow.

Lorenzo Snow received a revelation in 1899, emphasizing the importance of tithing in the Mormon Church. This revelation has now created great wealth in the church, with all members required to pay a ten percent tithe to the church prior to temple eligibility. Only a few years after attaining the Presidency, Lorenzo Snow passed away. Joseph F. Smith then became the President of the church in 1901, followed by Heber Grant in 1918, and George Albert Smith in 1945.

By 1947, the Mormon Church had grown to 1 million members. In 1950, early morning seminary began for all high-school students. This was an early morning bible study, aimed at teaching high school students the Mormon faith and is still a practice instituted today. In 1951, David McKay became the President of the church, and by 1963 the Mormon Church membership had doubled to 2 million members.

Less than 10 years later, under the leadership of President Joseph Fielding Smith, the church had grown to 3 million members. In July of 1972, Harold B. Lee was appointed President of the Church. He passed away a few months later in December of 1973, leaving Spencer W. Kimball to resume leadership. Within eight years, the church grew to 4 million members.

1978 was another important year in the Mormon faith. Still a tumultuous time in the Civil Rights movement, Spencer W. Kimball received a revelation authorizing the priesthood to all male members, regardless of race. This revelation is outlined in the Doctrine & Covenants, Official Declaration Two. Shortly thereafter, a new Latter-day Saint version of the King James Bible was published.

Ezra Taft Benson became the President in 1985, shortly after the Mormon Church membership reached 5 million people. Ezra Benson died in 1994, leaving the presidency to Howard Hunter, and then to Gordon B. Hinckley. Gordon Hinckley is still the president of the Mormon Church to this day.

Under President Hinckley, the Mormon Church began manufacturing the nutritional supplement Atmit for people suffering in the Ethiopian famine – and it is still produced for famine-stricken countries today.

Throughout the history of the LDS church, particularly in the early days of establishment, the early church leaders would give speeches. Those speeches were transcribed by members of the church, and later published into what would be known as the Journal of Discourses. Admittedly, I was never taught from the Journal of Discourses in my youth, likely because Mormons have abandoned most of the early church's teachings illustrated in these records due to their inflammatory subject matter. More information regarding the contents of these journals can be seen later in this book.

By 2006, membership had grown to 12 million people and the total continues to grow to this day. The LDS church has youthful beginnings – from the age of the church itself to the age of its very young leader. It has grown immensely since its inception and has undergone many large changes and alterations to doctrine within that time. Perhaps a closer look at those doctrines and a review of what allows those changes to occur is in order.

The Mormon Word

It is impossible to completely understand the Mormon Church without first understanding the Mormon view of the Bible and their belief in Revelations, as these are the cornerstones of their faith. Contrary to popular belief, Mormons actually do believe in the Bible. Their commonly used version of the Bible is the King James Version written in old English, and not the newer translations available today. They do believe that the Bible was divinely inspired, written by prophets, and contains the gospel of Jesus Christ.

The Bible is Kinda Right

It is easy for mainstream Christians to look at their Bibles and say, "yes, this is the Word of God." It's what I believe, and it's what mainstream Christians believe too. But it is difficult to argue with Mormons, because they don't entirely disagree. They believe in the Bible to be the Word of God, but only to a certain point. So you could say that they believe in the Bible – kinda.

One of the most major points of argument against the LDS Church is their open belief that the Bible is not the entire and whole Word of God. This is a major point of argument for most mainstream Christians, whose beliefs are rooted in the Bible and turn to only the Bible in questions of faith. Mormons believe that just as there have been prophets in the history of the world, there are also living prophets today.

They also believe that the Bible has undergone many, many translations and transcriptions over the course of time, and that while the Bible remains mostly complete, there are several points of doctrine that have been altered or omitted on occasion and interpreted by those in power.

This claim is a direct attack on early mainstream Christianity and the establishment of common beliefs by councils such as the Nicene council.

They further believe that Joseph Smith was able to restore these changes and provide a more correct version of salvation than any other available today.

Beyond the Bible, Mormons also believe that there are several other Scriptures that are just as literal and just as sacred. The eighth Article of Faith in the Mormon Church reads, "We believe the Bible to be the word of God as far as it is translated correctly; we also believe the Book of Mormon to be the word of God." Those other scriptures include the Book of Mormon, the Doctrine & Covenants, and the Pearl of Great Price.

A Lesson in American History

The Book of Mormon is considered to be a record of people in ancient America, engraved upon sheets of metal. Similar to the ancient prophets in the Bible, Mormons believe that there were also ancient prophets in America who prophesized and had revelations.

They believe that Jesus Christ came to the Americas and ministered personally to those people after his resurrection, just as he did to the Apostles of the old world. The result of those revelations and visits from Jesus were written in the Book of Mormon, outlining God's plan of salvation and telling people what they must do to gain eternal salvation and peace.

The Book of Mormon is an account of two separate nations. The first descended to America from Jerusalem in 600BC, and later separated into two nations – the Nephites and the Lamanites. "The other came much earlier when the Lord confounded tongues at the Tower of Babel" Book of Mormon, Introduction. These people were called the Jaredites. After the next thousand years, the only people left were the Lamanites. Mormons believe that the Lamanites are the ancient ancestors of the American Indians.

The Book of Mormon was told to be comprised of four types of metal record plates: The plates of Nephi, the Plates of Mormon, the Plates of Ether and the Plates of Brass. The Plates of Nephi were comprised of small and large plates, the small plates discussing the spiritual teachings of the prophets and the large plates providing a secular history of the people.

The Plates of Mormon were a synopsis of the Large Plates of Nephi, along with a continuation of the history written by Mormon. You will often hear Mormons speak of 'Moroni', who we introduced in the history of the church. The Angel Moroni stands at the top of all Mormon temples, Moroni being the son of Mormon and having written some additions to the Plates of Mormon. Moroni was the last of the Nephite prophets.

The Plates of Ether are a history of the Jaredites, a record condensed by Moroni who inserted comments of his own and compiled this history, calling it the Book of Ether. The Plates of Brass were brought by the people of Lehi from Jerusalem in 600 B.C., and contained "the five books of Moses . . . a record of the Jews from the beginning . . . down to the commencement of the reign of Zedekiah, king of Judah". This book also included the prophecies of the holy prophets.

The term 'Mormon' was coined after a prophet-historian named Mormon, attributed with quoting and abridging these golden plates, created the Book of Mormon as it is today. Once Mormon finished his writing, he gave the golden plates to his son Moroni. Moroni added his words to the golden plates before hiding them in the hill of Cumorah, where Joseph Smith would later find them as instructed by God.

Once Joseph Smith found the plates, it was Moroni who appeared to him and helped him translate the golden plates into English. Joseph Smith even said, "…the Book of Mormon was the most correct of any book on earth, and the keystone of our religion, and a man would get nearer to God by abiding by its precepts, than by any other book" Book of Mormon, Introduction. In that way, Joseph has elevated the Book of Mormon above the Bible, as a more correct interpretation of God's word.

If you ask a Mormon even today, they will likely tell you that they believe the Book of Mormon to be the most correct and true Word of God, even more so than the Bible. There were eleven witnesses who were said to be allowed to see the golden plates, though they did not have the power to read their inscriptions. After the golden plates had been interpreted by Joseph

Smith, the Mormon Church claims that Moroni sealed the sacred record and gave it to the Lord, to bring it back to the world later.

The Lesson that Keeps on Going

Further to the acknowledgement of the Book of Mormon, the Prophet Joseph continued to receive revelations from God, directing the 'restoration' of the Church. These revelations inspired the Doctrine and Covenants, as well as the Pearl of Great Price. The sixth Article of Faith states, "We believe in the same organization that existed in the Primitive Church, namely, apostles, prophets, pastors, teachers, evangelists, and so forth." The seventh Article of Faith furthers this point, stating "We belief in the gift of tongues, prophecy, revelation, visions, healing, interpretation of tongues and so forth."

The Doctrine and Covenants is actually a 'collection of divine revelations and inspired declarations' primarily written by the Prophet Joseph Smith, but also issued through other successors to the Presidency of the Church. These revelations and declarations are a compilation of warnings and messages for Church members, which are to be heeded for everlasting salvation. The ninth Article of Faith states, "We believe all that God has revealed, all that He does now reveal, and we believe that He will yet reveal many great and important things pertaining to the Kingdom of God." The Doctrine and Covenants is unique, as it is not a translation of ancient documentation, but it is actually a modern, living document that can be modified by living prophets.

A Random Assortment of Mormon Truths

The Pearl of Great Price is the fourth book in the Mormon repertoire. It is actually a selection of certain materials that touch on important aspects of the faith of the LDS church. I would consider this to be more of a life book than any of the others. The purpose of this fourth book was to make certain important articles which were limited in circulation more widely available and accessible to members of the church. Included in this book are the Thirteen Articles of Faith, and the History of the Church.

Once these four scriptures were prepared and completed, Joseph Smith received a revelation that these books were to be made into scripture. "...I have commanded you to organize yourselves, even to print my words, the fullness of my scriptures, the revelations which I have given unto you, and which I shall, hereafter, from time to time give unto you – for the purpose of building up my church and kingdom on the earth, and to prepare my people for the time when I shall dwell with them, which is nigh at hand" Doctrine & Covenants 104:58-59. Joseph compiled all of this documentation and created the new Mormon scriptures.

Once I turned eight years old and was baptized, my parents bought me my first set of Mormon scriptures. Typically, you will not see Mormons purchase each of these four books separately. They will purchase them the way I had mine – in a four-pack. All four scriptures are bound into one book, creating uniformity and the appearance of the one scripture as the entirety of the word of God.

Most mainstream Christian churches are teaching churches, meaning there are few restrictions regarding who can spread the Word of God. In Mormonism, this is not the case. In fact, to spread the Mormon word, you must first be deemed to have the authority to do so. "An again I say unto you that it shall not be given to anyone to go forth and preach my gospel, or to build up my church, except he be ordained by someone who has authority, and it is known to the church that he has authority and has been regularly ordained by the heads of the church. And again, the elders, priests and teachers of this church shall teach the principles of my gospel, which are in the Bible and the Book of Mormon, in which is the fullness for the gospel" Doctrine & Covenants 42:11-12.

As you can see in this verse, only those people who have the authority to each the Book of Mormon or the Bible are allowed to spread its word. It is also interesting since women are not ordained with authority as men of the church are, they are not permitted to teach the gospel and administer sacraments at the lengths that their male counterparts can.

Damned if you Don't

Growing up in the LDS church, I knew that following the rules in the Mormon scriptures and imposed by Mormon leaders was necessary. The Book of Mormon is the law of the Mormon church, so much so that the Doctrine & Covenants 42:59-60 even identifies it as a law and damns those who do not follow it, "Thou shalt take the things which thou has received, which have been given unto thee in my scriptures for a law, to be my law to govern my church. And he that doeth according to these things shall be saved, and he that doeth them not shall be damned if he so continue."

The Book of Mormon is law in the Mormon Church, and we were taught that you would be literally damned if you did not heed its words. It is important to note that in this Mormon directive, you must perform an action to attain salvation. This is in direct opposition to the Christian principle of grace, which will be discussed later.

Mormons believe that those who deny the words presented in the Book of Mormon are tempted by Satan, and simply afraid of being persecuted by their peers. "And he received the word with gladness, but straightway Satan tempted him; and the fear of persecution and the cares of the world caused him to reject the word" Doctrine & Covenants 40:2. Many people feel this way about religion – people are willing to forego their beliefs in order to fit into the mainstream religion of their peers.

For Mormons, any person falling away or rejecting the Mormon faith is doing so as a result of temptations from Satan. My own family members feel that this is the case with me, as I have turned by back on Mormonism and found my way into grace through mainstream Christianity.

While I can agree with the statement that people tend to fall away from their faith to do what is popular, I would also argue that Mormons tend to stay in their religion for the same reason. It is unpopular with church members and family members to leave the church, so they stay to keep others happy. What ultimately mattered to me was my relationship with God directly, and not my relationship with the LDS church.

Mormons will contend that the information in their three additional scriptures is not only the word of God, but the new requirements for Christianity and Salvation. "Behold, I say unto you that all old covenants have I caused to be done away in this thing; and this is a new and an everlasting covenant, even that which was from the beginning. Wherefore, although a man should be baptized a hundred times, it availeth him nothing, for you cannot enter in at the straight gate by the law of Moses, neither by your dead works" Doctrine & Covenants 22:1-2.

To me, these verses indicate that Mormons believe that their word is of divine inspiration, and overshadows anything written or contradictory in the Bible. There is nothing you can do outside of following the Mormon Doctrine to gain access to heaven.

To people of the Mormon faith, the Book of Mormon, Doctrine & Covenants, Bible, and Pearl of Great Price are all considered in the Mormon faith to be the 'corrected' words of God. It is important to understand the history and content of these doctrines and teachings, as found in these three additional scriptures. Their words are powerful and greatly influence and sometimes entirely alter the beliefs of the Mormon Church. Their philosophies can change as revelations prompt such change, and as the word of God, Mormons have no choice but to follow in the footsteps of their leaders.

THE ABSENCE OF EVIDENCE

The Mormon faith is centered on the Book of Mormon. In the Introduction of the Book of Mormon, this scripture is identified as a document that is comparable to the Bible. It is defined as a record of the ancient prophets and people in America, and the coming of Jesus to America. This doctrine is considered by Mormons to be the most correct scripture ever written, even more correct and important in nature than the Bible.

As we said before, the Mormons believe that the golden plates on which the Book of Mormon was written were sealed up by God, to be held in heaven until God decided to bring them back to the earth. If that is true, then Mormons are correct in saying that we should not find the golden plates here on earth. However, if the Book of Mormon is a true and sincere record of the people of America, we should be able to find archaeological evidence of the existence of the major civilizations spoken about in these records.

Care to Vacation in a Biblical City?

Over the course of centuries, archaeologists have set out to prove the literal, physical existence of the characters and locations mentioned in the Bible. There are dozens of cities mentioned throughout the Bible, many of which are still in existence today. Nazareth, Jordan, the Sea of Galilee, the Dead Sea, Jerusalem, Caper'naum, Be'er Sheva, Bethsaida, Bet She'an, the City of David and Jericho are amongst some of the many landmarks of the old world mentioned in the Bible which are still in existence today.

You can go to Jerusalem. You can take a trip to see the Dead Sea. These locations have been continuously settled for thousands of years, and the residents there have passed down these names from generation to generation. There is little question that these cities mentioned in the Bible did, and still do in many cases, exist.

Furthermore, there have been archaeological findings that are consistent with the Bible. For example, we have found coins, ruins, tunnels, and skeletal remains from battles spoken of in the Bible. The remains of Peter's home in Capernaum have been discovered. An ancient flight of stairs leading down to the Brook Kidron, as said to be used by Jesus and His disciples going to Gethsemane at the base of the Mount of Olives, was found in Caesarea and has been excavated. Granted, not every single instance in the Bible has been linked with archaeological findings as of yet.

However, the findings are consistent and undoubtedly connected with the Bible and thus the excavation and research continues. In many ways, the Bible has been used both as a historical document and as a map by scientists and anthropologists all over the world.

A Brief Recap of Mormon History

Let's go back to the contents of the Book of Mormon. As we said before, there were three groups of people in the Book of Mormon – Jaredites, Nephites and Lamanites. These were not small civilizations. The Jaredites were even foretold in Ether 1:43 to be the greatest civilization that would ever exist, "And there shall be none greater than the nation which I will raise up unto me of thy seed, upon all the face of the earth."

This was a prophecy, however, that would not come true even within the Book of Mormon. In fact, millions of Jaredites were killed in combat when the Jaredite nation was said to destroyed itself. In Ether 15:2, it said "He saw that there had been slain by the sword already nearly two millions of his people, and he began to sorrow in his heart; yea, there had been slain two millions of mighty men, and also their wives and children."

According to the Mormon scripture, this great battle of the Jaredites took place on the Hill Cumorah. After the destruction of the Jaredites and around 600BC, the Book of Mormon explains that two new great empires arose – the Nephites and the Lamanites. The Nephites were said to be fair skinned and the Lamanites were dark skinned because of their disobedience to God. These two civilizations also battled at the great Hill Cumorah once again, where the Lamanites destroyed the Nephites, all except one man – Moroni. "And my father also was killed by them, and I even remain alone to write the sad tale of the destruction of my people. But behold, they are gone, and I fulfill the commandment of my father" Mormon 8:3. Over 200,000 men were said to have died in this battle, by the Book of Mormon's own record. Before Mormon was killed, he took the plates and hid them in the Hill Cumorah – the same place that over a thousand years later, Moroni would give them to Joseph Smith.

DNA Doesn't Lie

At the end of these battles, the only civilization said to be in existence was the Lamanites, who are ancestors of the American Indians. However, there is a point to be made here. The Lamanites were descendant of the son of Lehi, who brought his family from Jerusalem. If the Lamanites were of Israeli descent and they are now ancestors of the American Indians – as Mormons will state that they are – that would mean that the American Indians would also necessarily be of Israeli descent.

First, there is no evidence of the Israeli people in America at that time. There is no oral or written history provided by Israelis or Native Americans on this subject. Furthermore, there has been DNA research performed trying to formulate a link between American Indians and Jewish populations. In testing DNA, the Y-chromosome DNA is passed on only by the father, while the mitochondrial DNA is passed on by the mother.

Neither of these DNA types can be recombined. After testing more than 150 tribes from North, Central and South America, including over 5000 participants, 99.4% of these Native Americans have a mitochondrial DNA lineage from Asia. The other 0.6% of participants has European or African lineage, and that is after the discovery of the New World by Columbus.

What do the experts say? These DNA examinations were performed by Dr. Simon Southerton, a Molecular Biologist with a Ph.D. from the University of Sydney, Dr. Stephen L. Whittington, a Biological Anthropologist with a Ph.D. from Penn State University, and Dr. Dennis O'Rourke, a Molecular Anthropologist with a Ph.D. from the University of Kansas and current

Professor at the University of Utah. Obviously these people were both qualified and educated in their area of work. Through their research of Native American DNA, there have been zero cases of Hebrew DNA ever being found in the DNA of Native Americans. *Question: How did two massive empires exist, said to be descendant of the Israelites, when there is no biological linkage that can be found between people of Israel and people of early America? How can the Lamanites possibly be the ancestors of the Native Americans?*

Where have all the Cities Gone?

Going back to physical locations, the Book of Mormon suggests that the land occupied first by the Jaredites is along a narrow strip of land, most likely indicating Mesoamerica. In fact, Mormons readily admit that their inclination is that the people mentioned in the Book of Mormon were in all likelihood from Mesoamerica, today called Mexico and Guatemala. Within the Book of Mormon, there are stories of cities called Nephi, Manti, Zarahemla, Bountiful and Sidom.

Yet within the areas of Mesoamerica, there is literally zero history or record from any of the archaeological findings of these areas that these cities existed at all. *Question: Where are these cities in the Book of Mormon and why are there no records of their existence today? Why can I not visit places in the Book of Mormon, as I can the places of the Bible?* There are no records from neighboring city ruins that they existed in Mesoamerica, or had even been seen by cities in the area. In fact, there is no piece of land that fits the descriptions provided in the Book of Mormon entirely. It simply does not exist.

Where have all the People Gone?

Stranger yet is the great Hill Cumorah where Mormons believe that Joseph Smith found the gold plates. According to the Mormon Church, this Hill is actually in New York. How is it possible for these people to have existed in Mesoamerica, but fought a great battle thousands of miles away in New York?

The Book of Mormon does not explain this. If the battle did not occur on the Hill Cumorah and rather occurred somewhere else, then why did the Book of Mormon not speak the truth? *Question: How can the plates be in a location thousands of miles away from the homeland of millions of people?*

According to the Book of Mormon, there were "millions" of people exterminated in these two great battles, both said to have taken place on the Hill Cumorah. The Mormon Church has purchased most of the land on and around the Hill Cumorah, calling this location a historical church site. Okay, so let's give the book the benefit of the doubt. I'll go along with this and say that the Book of Mormon is right, and millions of people battled and died at the Hill Cumorah. *Question: Where are their bodies? Where are the mass graves and the skeletal remains of all of these people?*

There have been very few attempts at excavating the Hill Cumorah, performed many years ago. Nothing was found in those excavations. If the LDS church is so very confident that the Hill Cumorah is the location of such great battles and such innumerable deaths, it is interesting to note that they have not permitted the excavations that would prove their story correct. To me, this is an indication that they are trying to avoid a great embarrassment to the Mormon Church and their beliefs.

I have seen arguments where Mormons have said, "Do you have to dig up your grandmother to know she's in the ground?" To this, I answer, "No." But the burial site of my grandmother is not the cornerstone of an entire religion with 12 million followers, either. *Question: If the Mormons have nothing to hide, then why are they hiding it? Why will they not excavate the Hill Cumorah?*

If you don't believe me, here's a challenge for you. Call the Hill Cumorah Visitor's Center in Palmyra, New York. Confirm that this hill is the one mentioned in the Book of Mormon, and then ask them if there have been any discoveries made from any excavations, and if there were, where you could see those discoveries. Their answer will speak volumes.

Where did the Archaeological Evidence go?

Every single civilization that has existed on this planet has left some remnants of their existence. Graves, tombs, roads, coins, houses, temples, tunnels, you name it. People leave evidence of their lives and their history, creating an archaeological roadmap. Let's talk about metals. Metals of any form are some of the longest-lasting archaeological findings we have. They are durable and can withstand the test of time, not degrading or cracking as significantly as other materials might.

In 1 Nephi 18:25 it states, "And we did find all manner of ore, both of gold, and of silver, and of copper," speaking of the arrival of Lehi and his sons in the Promised Land. The footnote of this part of the Book of Mormon claims that this took place around 589BC. However, according to archaeological findings, metallurgy does not appear in the New World until several hundred years after Christ.

Likewise, the Book of Mormon also mentions other items created from metallurgy, including armor of war such as breastplates, helmets, shields and swords. In Alma 43:19 it says, "And when the armies of the Lamanites saw that the people of Nephi, or that Moroni, had prepared his people with breastplates and with arm-shields, yea, and also shields to defend their heads…", and in Mosiah 8:10-11 it says, "And behold, also, they have brought breastplates, which are large, and they are of brass and of copper, and are perfectly sound. And again, they have brought swords, the hilts thereof have perished, and the blades thereof were cankered with rust."

Even greater that the mention of these precious metals is the outright mention of steel in 1 Nephi 4:9, "And I beheld his sword, and I drew it forth from the sheath thereof; and the hilt thereof was of pure gold, and the workmanship thereof was exceedingly fine, and I saw that the blade thereof was of the most precious steel." To work with a product like steel would require smelting the metal, which would have most definitely left an archaeological indication of this early metalworking. The level of metallurgy described in the Book of Mormon was quite advanced.

Not only was their metallurgy advanced, but the Book of Mormon also mentions that they had horse-drawn chariots. In Alma 18: 9, both horses and chariots are mentioned, "Now the king had commanded his servants, previous to the time of the watering of their flocks, that they should prepare his horses and chariots…" First, evidence has proven that ancient Native Americans would have utilized products such as obsidian and flint to create primitive tools like arrowheads and knife blades. Second, the use of something as elaborate as a chariot would have also had some resounding evidence.

Yet there is absolutely zero archaeological evidence of any metal work such as smelting was performed, and no evidence that other well-studied ancient cultures witnessed anything as extravagant as horse drawn chariots. There is also zero evidence that Native Americans utilized swords at all. And there is zero evidence that there were chariots, let alone those drawn by horses (which is another issue entirely). *Question: If the Nephites and Lamanites fought with swords and full armor, and utilized chariots, why can modern-day archaeologists find zero evidence of their skeletal remains, or at least these metal-formed swords and body armors used in this battle? Why have they not been found at the Hill Cumorah?*

Just as the Book of Mormon mentions complicated metallurgy, they also mention the manufacturing of coins. Coins are mentioned throughout the Bible, and archaeological digs throughout the Middle East have found hundreds of coins dating back to Biblical civilizations. In the descriptive text of the Book of Mormon, Alma 11, it says, "Nephite coinage set forth." Now, not only did the Nephites have the ability to work with metals, but also the ability to cast coins. Metal currency is amongst the most durable and common artifacts found in archaeological digs.

If the ancient Americans utilized a coin system, it would be safe to assume that some of those coins would be found in archaeological excavations. However, again, this is not the case. There is zero evidence that any Native Americans ever even used metal currency, and those who did, did not do so until the Europeans settled in America and introduced them to the concept. *Question: Why have archaeologists never found evidence of the Nephite coinage mentioned in the Book of Mormon?*

Plants and Animals of the Past

There are many, many animals mentioned in the Bible, and all are accurate within the scope of time that they were mentioned. While there are references to animals such as lions that no longer exist in the modern-day areas of the Bible, there are some very early records that do indicate sightings of those animals during an appropriate time period. Let's compare this to the Book of Mormon.

It is a widely recognized scientific fact that prior to the European descent upon the Americas, several Old World species of animals did not exist in America. In fact, it was not until the sixteenth century AD that Europeans introduced horses, pigs and cows to the Native American people.

However, this is not how the Book of Mormon tells this story. Between 500BC and 589BC by their own records in 1 Nephi 18:25, "And it came to pass that we did find upon the land of promise, as we journeyed in the wilderness, that there were beasts in the forests of every kind, both the cow and the ox, and the ass and the horse, and the goat and the wild goat, and all manner of wild animals, which were for the use of men."

The elephant was not brought to America until the late 1700's. Yet in the Book of Mormon, Ether 9:18-19, it says "And also all manner of cattle, of oxen, and cows, and of sheep, and of swine, and of goats, and also many other kinds of animals which were useful for the food of man. And they also had horses, and asses, and there were elephants and cureloms and cumoms; all of which were useful to man, and more especially the elephants and cureloms and cumoms."

If indeed there were horses, cows, elephants and other animals that existed in ancient America, there should be archaeological evidence of those animals. There would be not only the skeletal remains of these large animals, but given the apparent usefulness of these animals, there would also be drawings and illustrations made by surrounding tribes and ancient people. Again, however, there is zero indication that elephants, horses, or many of those animals existed prior to the arrival of the Europeans in the New World. *Question: How could these animals exist but there be no skeletal, architectural, literary or illustrative reference to these animals of any kind?*

We all enjoy Thanksgiving every year in America, right? We feast and make reference to the foods enjoyed by Native Americans, including potatoes, tomatoes and squash. However, there are references in the Book of Mormon made to crops that we know factually were not brought to America until the arrival of the Europeans in the New World – namely barley and wheat.

In Alma 11:7, it says "A senum of silver was equal to a senine of gold, and either for a measure of barley, and also for a measure of every kind of grain." Again in Mosiah 7:22 barley is mentioned, "And behold, we at this time do pay tribute to the kind of the Lamanites, to the amount of one half of our corn, and our barley, and even our grain of every kind." Mosiah 9:9 mentions both barley and wheat, "And we began to till the ground, yea, even with all manner of seeds, with seeds of corn, and of wheat, and of barley, and with neas, and with sheum, and with seeds of all manner of fruits."

Now, these grains were most definitely part of the Old World, and were definitely mentioned within the Bible. They have their place in the Bible because they existed there at that time. *Question: How is it possible that ancient people grew these popular grains in abundance, but there is no archaeological evidence that these grains ever existed in any capacity in the New World prior to the arrival of the Europeans?*

The Great Conversion

In the Book of Mormon, Helamen 6:3, after the coming of Jesus to America there is a mention of a great conversion of all of the Lamanites to Christianity, "Nevertheless, the people of the church did have great joy because of the conversion of the Lamanites, yea, because of the church of God, which had been established among them, And they did fellowship on with one another, and did rejoice one with another, and did have great joy."

Had there been a massive conversion to Christianity in America, there would have been abundant evidence of this Christian worship. There would have been archaeological findings from not only these peoples, but of surrounding Native American tribes who also learned of Christianity. If these plates were the word of God and were worshipped by the ancient Americans, the religious leaders of the group would have made copies of these texts. *Question: Why is there no evidence of a massive conversion to Christianity in ancient America?*

Ancient Evidence of Scriptural Writings

The Dead Sea scrolls were a massive discovery decades ago, containing Biblical texts written in Hebrew, Aramaic and Greek and dating back to 150BC. They are some of the earliest evidence that exists of the Old Testament. As Christians, we can go and see the actual Dead Sea scrolls, hold them in our hands (well, probably not, I would imagine they are under lock and key), date them and be a witness to their existence. There are hundreds of manuscripts of the Greek New Testament, which have been studied all over the world. There are hundreds of physical, ancient documents that have been translated and verified by countless scholars.

This is not the case with the Book of Mormon. There are no manuscripts that can be reviewed, other than the original documents written by Joseph Smith. There are no metal plates which scholars can review for accuracy and content. While the Mormon Church maintains that these were sealed up to heaven until God decides to return them to the earth, I would argue that it is a fantastic cover-up for plates of gold which never existed at all. There is evidence everywhere of the Bible's existence in the Old World, but there is zero evidence of the Book of Mormon's existence in America. *Question: Why is it that God would choose not to hide up all of the contents and evidence of the Bible, but would choose to hide up the contents of the Book of Mormon?*

The people of the Book of Mormon are admittedly people very cultured in writing and reading. Helamen 3:15, "But behold, there are many books and many records of every kind, and they have been kept chiefly by the Nephites," and 3 Nephi 5:9 "But behold there are records which do contain all the proceedings of this people", these are both statements in the Book of Mormon indicating that this society was advanced and scholarly.

Furthermore, if their records were kept as the Book of Mormon was kept then it is likely that these records would have been written on plates of metal or rock. As such, they would be far more difficult to destroy than materials like paper. *Question: If these people kept books and extensive records of the happenings of their civilization, why can we find no evidence of these writings? Not even a single one?*

When looking at the cultured ancient American society discussed in the Book of Mormon, one must also examine how these people wrote and also the language of the people. Given that Lehi's family came from Jerusalem, it is interesting to note that in ancient America there is no evidence of Greek or Hebrew writings at all, as one might expect.

It is also strange that upon arriving in this Promised Land, Nephi would write the plates not in his native language, but in another language altogether. In Mormon 9:32, it says "And now, behold, we have written this record according to our knowledge, in the characters which are called among us the reformed Egyptian, being handed down and altered by us, according to our manner of speech."

First, there is no documented example of this reformed Egyptian writing. Mormons will argue that it was similar to Egyptian but different, and therefore it was 'reformed'. They compare this to how English is derived from Latin, and therefore English is just reformed Latin. I would argue that the difference between Egyptian and reformed Egyptian versus English as reformed Latin is that both English and Latin are recognized and documented languages.

Reformed Egyptian, whatever that may be, is not a documented or researched language and therefore is not considered a real language at all. If Mormons could provide any documentation at all of what reformed Egyptian is, perhaps the linguistic community would give this language some merit. Since no such documentation has ever been provided or studied as to confirm the authenticity of this language, reformed Egyptian is considered for all intensive purposes to be a made-up or fictional language. *Question: In a literary society such as those recorded in the Book of Mormon, why is there zero evidence of this reformed Egyptian, the apparent written language of hundreds of thousands of people?*

Proof of Your Existence

Aside from the writing itself, you must look at the people spoken of in the Bible. For example, the most popular man of the entire Bible – Jesus. There is little doubt in the scientific community that Jesus actually was a real man. There are many non-Christian texts that mention Jesus, namely written by the ancient Jewish community. While they did not approve of what Jesus spoke of, they still recognize His literal existence. Pagan Roman authors such as Conrelius Tacitus and Gaius Suetonius wrote secular documents referencing Jesus.

There were records of the names of High Priests of the early church, and burial evidence has been found linking chronologically accurate burial sites to those church records. There is overwhelming evidence on the side of Biblical Christianity that events from the Bible did occur and the people of the Bible did exist.

Before you can ask whether or not the prophets of the Book of Mormon spoke the truth, you must first ask yourself another very real question. *Question: Did the prophets spoken of in the Book of Mormon ever really exist?* There are no archaeological findings that have proven in any way that the prophets mentioned in the Book of Mormon ever existed at all. There are no burial sites, no written records of Christian or secular nature, and no physical evidence of any kind.

Throwing Down the Gauntlet

By making these statements, I have undoubtedly stirred some very strong accusations. However, Mormons claim that the Book of Mormon is similar in nature to the Bible, and even going as far as to say that it is the most correct book ever written. It is my opinion that this simply cannot be the case, for several reasons.

There is no evidence that the places of the Book of Mormon exist or ever did exist, no skeletal evidence of the bodies of over two million people, no DNA linkage between Israelites and Native Americans, no evidence of metallurgy of any kind including swords, armor and chariots, no evidence of coinage, no evidence of Old World animals or grains in the New World, no evidence of the golden plates of the Book of Mormon itself, no evidence of a massive conversion to Christianity in ancient America, no evidence of books or records written in reformed Egyptian, and no evidence that the prophets spoken of in the Book of Mormon ever existed at all. There is literally no evidence at all.

Mormons are encouraged to turn into their hearts when facing these affronts to their faith. They are told that it is an act of faith to believe in these things, even though they have no evidence that they exist at all. Not believing in the stories or even raising these questions of the Book of Mormon is considered anti-Mormon, an affront to their living prophet, and a rejection of the faith.

To hear more perspectives and information about the historical and archaeological absence of evidence in the Book of Mormon, I would encourage you to view a video called *The Bible vs. the Book of Mormon*, compiled by Living Hope Ministries in Brigham, Utah. Coming from a city nearly entirely inhabited by Mormons, they have a unique perspective on this religion. The archaeologists in the film were actually Mormons who set out to prove that the Book of Mormon was historically accurate, but in fact found that it was not. It is a very informative, factually-based video that speaks about many of the same issues I had brought up in this chapter, and I would highly recommend you view it yourself or show it to a Mormon friend.

Church Hierarchy

The Mormon Church has over 12 million members, with around 50,000 missionaries serving around the globe. Before we can dig too deep into the Mormon Church and their beliefs, it is important to understand the Church structure. The Mormon Church is meticulous in its organization, making every Church nearly identical and the structure seamless across the globe. This level of organization has promoted their growth and their wealth over time.

The Leaders of the Pack

Most mainstream Christian Churches are led by a Pastor, who in many cases carries with him an advanced degree and several years of training and Bible study prior to ever becoming a Pastor. The Mormon Church, on the other hand, is led by a President, also known as the Prophet. Doctrine & Covenants 107:91-92 states, "And again, the duty of the President of the office of the High Priesthood is to preside over the whole church, and to be like unto Moses – behold, here is wisdom; yea, to be a seer, a revelator, a translator, and a prophet, having all the gifts of God which he bestows upon the head of the church."

The President of the church can receive revelations from God required to lead the LDS Church forward, and will serve a life term. It is the Prophet of the Mormon Church who is said to hold the keys of the kingdom of God, "Unto whom I have given the keys of the kingdom, which belong always unto the Presidency of the High Priesthood" Doctrine & Covenants 81:2. To follow in the Mormon Prophet's teachings is to follow the Prophet to the kingdom of God, as he is the only holder of those keys. Alongside the President are his two Counselors, also believed to have the ability to prophesize. Together, the President and his two Counselors form the First Presidency.

Beneath the President of the Church resides the Quorum of the Twelve Apostles. It is important to note that, as in many churches, only men are allowed to hold these high-level positions within the Church. The Twelve Apostles are twelve men, also believed to have some prophetic abilities. The Quorum of the Twelve Apostles along with the First Presidency will oversee the administrative needs of the Mormon Church globally. The Quorum will also elect the next President to the LDS Church, but historically it is the Apostle who has served in the Quorum the longest who is elected to be the President and Prophet.

The Apostles of the Mormon Church have several responsibilities, including, "calling to baptize; and to ordain other elders, priests, teachers and deacons; and to administer bread and wine – the emblems of the flesh and blood of Christ – and to confirm those who are baptized into the church, by the laying on of hands for the baptism of fire and the Holy Ghost, according to the scriptures; and to teach, expound, exhort, baptize and watch over the church; and to confirm the church by the laying on of hands, and giving of the Holy Ghost; and to take the lead of all meetings" Doctrine & Covenants 20:38-44. The Apostles are called to tend to the church and its people in all of these ways, and are called upon to be leaders within it.

Beneath the Twelve Apostles is the 70's Quorum. It is important to be able to lead the Church globally, and understanding this need has been fundamental to the Mormon Church's stronghold both in the United States and the world. There are five Quorums of the Seventy, and these five Quorums are led by Presidency of the Seventy. The Presidency of the Seventy is comprised of seven male members of the Quorums of the Seventy. The First and Second Quorums of the Seventy are similar in nature to the Twelve Apostles and have the authority to preside over any region of the world. The Third, Fourth and Fifth Quorums of the Seventy are more limited in authority, and are only granted power within their pre-designated area.

Stakes & Wards

Beneath these Quorums are called Stakes. Each Stake will be under the authority of a Stake President and two Counselors, again very similar to the structure of the First Presidency. An average Stake will have about 3,000 members. These members are divided into between five and twelve different wards or branches, dependent upon their size. Larger groups would be considered Wards, while small groups are considered Branches. When you go to church on a typical Sunday morning, the people who attend church with you would be considered members of your ward. However, even the wards are strictly structured. Based on your geographical location and proximity to the Church, you will attend a specific service or ward appointed to you at a specific time.

All people from that geographical location will always have Church together, ideally building somewhat of a Church family and fellowship amongst the members of a Ward. Growing up in the LDS church, we very rarely changed the boundary lines for wards. Typically, the only reason for a boundary line change would be the building of a new Church.

Each ward is assigned a Bishop, which would be analogous to a Pastor but much less rigorous to attain. It should be noted that most Bishops do not perform their leadership exclusively. When I began attending a mainstream Christian church, I thought it was the strangest thing that being a Pastor was a job. I had never in my life been to a church where a church leader considered their duties at church to be an occupation.

In the LDS church, a Bishop is typically a member of the ward, selected through revelation by leaders of the church to lead the people of that ward. They often have a secular job, wife and family aside from their responsibilities at the church. While bishops will have served on a mission and trained to go on their mission, they have little formal training on the scriptures. This is unlike most mainstream Christian Pastors who are required to go to seminary, hold a college degree and have formal religious training and education.

Again, similar to the First Presidency, the Bishop is given two male Counselors on which to rely. Together, these three men make the Bishopric and are responsible for all ward organizations, functions and programs. They will together handle the administrative needs of the ward, as well as the spiritual, emotional and physical needs of its members.

Men & the Priesthood

Within the Ward, there are varying levels of what is called 'priesthood'. The Aaronic Priesthood is bestowed upon young male members of the church beginning at the age of twelve. This is the Priesthood of Aaron, shown in Doctrine & Covenants 13:1, "Upon you my fellow servants, in the name of the Messiah I confer the Priesthood of Aaron, which holds the keys of the ministering of angels, and the gospel of repentance, and of baptism by immersion for the remission of sins; and this shall never be taken again from the earth, until the sons of Levi do offer again and offering unto the Lord in righteousness." Between ages twelve and seventeen, young men with the Aaronic Priesthood receive opportunities to participate in sacred priesthood ordinances, along with service opportunities. Women are not allowed to hold any priesthood powers of any kind.

Contained in the Aaronic Priesthood are four offices - Bishops (not to be confused with the Bishop position that is the head of the Ward), Priests, Teachers and Deacons. These positions such as priests and teachers have their own meaning in the Mormon hierarchy, and should not be confused with the terminology as we understand it. The first level is the Deacon, who typically passes out the Sacrament (similar to communion) to church members. The responsibilities of Deacons are very limited. Per Doctrine & Covenants 20:57-59, Teachers are to be "…assisted always, in all his duties in the church, by the deacons, if occasion requires. But neither teachers nor deacons have authority to baptize, administer the sacrament, or lay on hands; they are however, to warn, expound, exhort and teach, and invite all to come unto Christ."

Teachers are the second level and can perform the same duties as Deacons, but also have the responsibility preparing (but not blessing) the sacrament before it is passed to members of the congregation, as well as serving as home teachers. "The teacher's duty is to watch over the church always, and be with and strengthen them; and see that there is no iniquity in the church, neither hardness with each other, neither lying, backbiting, nor evil speaking; and see that the church meet together often, and also see that all the members do their duty. And he is to take the lead of meetings in the absence of the elder or priest" Doctrine & Covenants 20: 53-56.

Priests are the third level of the Aaronic Priesthood and may perform the duties of both Deacons and Teachers. However, they also have the added duties of blessing the Sacrament, baptizing, and ordaining others to the offices of Priest, Teacher and Deacon.

The Bishop is considered to be the President of the Aaronic Priesthood, and will oversee and delegate responsibilities to the Aaronic Priesthood members through the Bishopric, of which he is the head. As Doctrine & Covenants 20:46-49 states, "The priest's duty is to preach, teach, expound, exhort, and baptize, and administer the sacrament, and visit the house of each member, and exhort them to pray vocally and in secret and attend to all family duties. And he may also ordain other priests, teachers, and deacons. And he is to take the lead of meetings when there is no elder present. But when there is an elder present, he is only to preach, expound, exhort and baptize."

The Aaronic Priesthood is considered a preparation for the next step of priesthood, or as the Doctrine & Covenants 107:14 states, "it is an appendage to the greater, or the Melchizedek Priesthood, and has power in administering outward ordinances." Upon turning the age of eighteen, young men of the church are eligible to gain the authority of the Melchizedek Priesthood. At this level, church leaders are able to direct these young men to preach the gospel of the Mormon Church around the world.

The Mormon Church maintains that this Melchizedek Priesthood was given to Adam and was on the earth when God created the Bible, but God removed it during the apostasy – when people turned away from the gospel and corrupted its principles by making unauthorized changes upon the death of Jesus. They also maintain that the Melchizedek Priesthood was restored when the Apostles Peter, James and John came to Joseph Smith and Oliver Cowdery and conferred it upon them.

Within the Melchizedek Priesthood, there are five different levels. These include Apostle, Seventy, Patriarch, High Priest and Elder. However, there are several requirements prior to sustaining any office within the Mormon Church. Permission must be granted by a member who has the authority to appoint people to offices within the church, and has been ordained as such by the leaders of the Church. Men who gain these different titles within the church are granted the corresponding different levels of priesthood 'keys', or access to perform certain works.

In Doctrine & Covenants 20:42, "Elders in the church are called to teach, expound, exhort, baptize and watch over the Church; and to confirm the church by the laying on of hands, and giving of the Holy Ghost." All men holding the Melchizedek Priesthood are considered to be Elders, and will conduct the meetings of the church when there is no High Priest present. A High Priest has the "authority to administer in spiritual things" as is dictated in the Doctrine & Covenants 107:12. The High Priests have the power to ordain stake and mission presidents, high councilors, bishoprics and other leaders of the church.

The Council of the Twelve Apostles will authorize a Stake President to ordain a Patriarch. A Patriarch is selected to be a person who will give special patriarchal blessings to members of the Mormon Church. Patriarchal blessings typically include a declaration of lineage. This declaration of ancestry affirms that the person is a descendant of Abraham, belonging to a specific 'tribe of Jacob'. Many LDS members are also said to be of the 'tribe of Ephraim'. Mormons maintain that since we have many bloodlines running in each of us, it is possible that two members from the same family could be declared as being from different tribes in Israel.

While I do not see how this is possible so long as siblings come from the same parents, the LDS church maintains that this is true. Church members also maintain that whether they are a descendant of Abraham by bloodline or adoption, are all equally descendants of Abraham and therefore heir to the promises of the Abrahamic Covenant. Long story short, everyone can be heir to the promises of this covenant. While we will discuss these blessings later in this book, they are in essence blessings that will explain our callings on earth and are interpreted by the Mormon Church to be God's word directly to us. Patriarchs are also considered to be High Priests.

The Melchizedek Priesthood also includes the 70's Quorum. The Seventies are considered special witnesses of Jesus Christ to the world, and are instructed to build up and regulate the church in this position. The Doctrine & Covenants 107:25 states, "The Seventy are also called to preach the gospel, and to be especial witnesses unto the Gentiles and in all the world – thus differing from other officers in the church in the duties of their calling.

The last group, of course, is the Apostles. These men are called to the highest office of Apostle in the Melchizedek Priesthood and are part of the Quorum of the Twelve. They hold all of the priesthood keys, though only the President and Prophet can actively exercise all of the keys. As stated earlier, it is typically the eldest member of the Quorum of the Twelve who will take leadership of the Mormon Church as president and prophet, upon the death of the existing leader.

Women in the Church

Of course, in all of this you may be wondering where the women's role in the church lies. The structure for the women of the Mormon Church is quite different than that set out for the men of the church. This program, just like the Young Men's program presented for the men of the church, is called the Young Women's program. Having been a member of this program myself, I can attest to the differences in these programs.

The Young Men's program is a preparation – a staircase upon which men can start at the bottom, and make spiritual progressions to higher and higher levels within the church. Since women do not hold power to progress up the staircase within the church, the Young Women's program is more of an activities bureau. In fact, the group was actually created as a result of the then President of the Church, Brigham Young, desiring for his daughters to be more conservative.

Per the November 2003 *New Era Magazine* article (an official LDS endorsed magazine) entitled '134 Years Young'; they stated that in 1869 "President Brigham Young is concerned about the young women in the Church. He is worried that some of them, including his own daughters, are too caught up in the fashions or trends of the world...At first, this is difficult for his daughters...Now they can't spend hours looking at clothing catalogs from back East. Instead they must sew their own simple and modest dresses, without any ruffles, that go all the way to the ground. They must spend less time socializing and more time studying the scriptures and learning the gospel. But these girls know their father is a prophet, and they choose to follow him. They create the Young Ladies Department of the Cooperative Retrenchment Association and begin meeting often to support each other in their efforts."

Of course, these standards have been slightly relaxed and women do not have to sew their own clothes anymore. But this was the beginning of the strict modesty that you still find today within the Mormon Church, a level of modesty that I can recall personally. This also begins to illustrate the role of women within the Church. Like the Young Men's program, the Young Women's program allows for some progression based upon age.

Upon the age of twelve, Young Women join the Beehives. From ages fourteen to fifteen, women become Mia Maids – which are called such because of the initials of the Mutual Improvement Association. The eldest groups of Young Women, from ages sixteen to seventeen, are called Laurels. It is important to distinguish that there are few spiritual blessings or powers passed on to women in the church. The activities in Young Women's groups are primarily service and fellowship driven, promoting positive activities to keep the women of the church engaged in non-secular activities.

After the age of 18, women join the Relief Society. In a 1976 article of *Ensign Magazine* (also an official LDS-endorsed magazine) entitled 'Relief Society – Its Promise and Potential', President Spencer W. Kimball says, "The Relief Society is the Lord's organization for women. It complements the priesthood training given to the brethren." Upon the age of 18, women join this society and will volunteer to be teachers of classes or organizations within the church. The President of the Relief Society is able to receive revelations for those within their Relief Society group.

One major aspect of the Relief Society is Visiting Teaching. Visiting Teaching is simply ministering at the home of another Relief Society member. As Julie Beck states in the November 2009 issue of *Ensign Magazine* in the article 'Relief Society: A Sacred Work', "This is the Lord's program of individual watchcare for His daughters, the policies regarding visiting teaching are approved by the First Presidency as outlined in the Church Handbook of Instructions." As I mentioned earlier, it is the Bishop of every church who is responsible for looking after the needs of his ward. Later in Julie Beck's article, she says, "...the Bishop and the Relief Society president have the responsibility to receive revelation as to who should be assigned to watch over and strengthen each individual sister...we demonstrate our faith and follow a pattern established by the Lord as we report on our assignment every month."

Involuntarily Voluntary Positions

Participating in these programs is not sincerely a voluntary act within the LDS church. Mormons believe that participation in these programs furthers their progression towards salvation. The means by which people are ordained into new offices is also a very public and important matter within the Mormon Church. Mormons often hold conferences at many levels – stake conferences, or even the entire church body at General Conference – to hold votes and ordain people into new offices.

"Each priest, teacher, or deacon, who is ordained by a priest, may take a certificate from him at the time, which certificate, when presented to an elder, shall entitle him to a license, which shall authorize him to perform the duties of his calling, or he may receive it from a conference. No person is to be ordained to any office in this church, where there is a regularly organized branch of the same, without the vote of the church." Doctrine & Covenants 20:64.

As a child, I do recall all the people of the church voting and ordaining people into new offices. They would ask the congregation to raise their right hand to signify that they agree that the person in question should be promoted to a new office of the church, and then ask if any opposed. I also recall that no one ever opposed the vote. I tried to oppose a vote one time when I was about eight years old to see what would happen, but my mother grabbed my hand and shoved it in my lap, giving me the look of death for a moment. Needless to say, I didn't do that again.

The record of every single member, and their active or inactive status, is kept on record at the Mormon Church. Each ward provides "…a list of the names of the several members uniting themselves with the church since the last conference…so the names of the whole church may be kept in a book by one of the elders, whomsoever the other elders shall appoint from time to time; and also, if any have been expelled from the church, so that their names may be blotted out of the general church record of names" Doctrine & Covenants 20:82-83.

The Nature of God

The first Article of Faith states that Mormons believe in God, the Eternal Father, and in His Son, Jesus Christ, and in the Holy Ghost. It is important to clarify that Mormons do not believe in the Trinity the way that most people of the Christian faith believe in the Trinity, as described in the Nicene Creed. Webster's dictionary defines the Trinity as "the unity of Father, Son and Holy Spirit as three persons in one Godhead according to Christian dogma", where dogma means an established opinion.

For the purposes of this book (and hopefully the agreement of most Christians), believing in the Trinity is belief that we worship one God in three persons. The three persons are God the Father, Jesus Christ, and the Holy Spirit. While these are three distinct persons, they are of one divine essence and that essence is God.

Trinity Troubles

The Trinity has long been one of the most confusing aspects of Christianity. It is difficult for us to rationalize that Jesus, God and the Holy Spirit are three in one. For me, growing up in the LDS church made comprehending the Trinity as an adult to be even more complex, as the fundamentals of Mormonism and the nature of God are very different than the mainstream consensus on the subject. I had no idea what the Trinity was until I attended a mainstream Christian Church. I knew I had heard of it before, but I did not know what it was. In fact, up until attending that Christian Church, I had no idea that Mormons believed any differently than other Christians.

In the Mormon Church, probably more often than others, you will often hear people refer to God more often as our Heavenly Father than as God. While Mormons believe in God, Jesus Christ and the Holy Ghost, they believe in these things very differently.

To them, God is our Heavenly Father and Creator, Jesus Christ is the literal son of God, and the Holy Ghost is a spirit sent by God to teach truth and comfort His people. To this end, they do not believe that they are of one essence, but rather entirely separate beings.

This concept is understandably confusing, as the interpretation of the Bible is where this comes into play. At some points in the LDS church, they will take versus from the Bible literally and at other times take them figuratively. There are several places where the Bible distinctly mentions the oneness of God. For example, John 17:22 says "And the glory which thou gavest me I have given them; that they may be one, even as we are one."

In mainstream Christianity, this is a literal statement, meaning that God and Jesus are one. Again this is said in Deuteronomy 6:4, saying, "Hear, O Israel: The Lord our God is one Lord", and repeated again in Mark 12:29, "Hear, O Israel: The Lord our God is one Lord."

Even further this is mentioned in Philippians 2:11 "and that every tongue should confess that Jesus Christ is Lord, to the glory of God the Father," and again in John 14:9, when he says "He that hath seen me hath seen the Father." The Holy Spirit is also mentioned to be of oneness with God in 2 Corinthians 3:17 "Now the Lord is that Spirit, and where the Spirit of the Lord is, there is liberty." Here there are six verses, all pointing to the oneness of God. To interject a personal opinion, it seems that God tends to repeat himself when things are really important.

It has been the view of mainstream Christianity that these verses are literal, and if Jesus is God, and the Lord is Holy Spirit, then all three must be one. To me, the best example given to me was a family. The wife, husband and child are all three separate individuals, but they are still one family. Another example would be water. Water can be a solid, a liquid and a gas – but it is still water. The mainstream Christian view of the Trinity is just like this, where Heavenly Father, Jesus and the Holy Spirit are three separate and distinct entities, yet they are still one God.

The Mormon interpretation of these statements is not literal. They say that God, the Holy Spirit and Jesus, while being physically separate, are still united in purpose and thought. The oneness is a concept, not a literal truth.

Mormons believe that Jesus is not God. The Holy Spirit is not God. God is God. They are all independent of one another, and therefore there is no such thing as the Trinity as defined by most mainstream Christians. For these reasons, the LDS church refers to the Trinity in a different way, calling this the Godhead. Now, the term Godhead is not unique to the Mormon Church and is used in mainstream Christian Churches as well, so do not confuse the Godhead as it is known in mainstream Christianity with the term as it is used by the Mormon Church.

Just know that you will never hear a person of LDS faith refer to the Trinity and that their view of the Godhead would not be the same as a Godhead reference outside of the Mormon Church. Their Godhead is the similar to the Trinity in personages, yet completely different in interpretation of the oneness of God.

Where do they cite this in the Bible? It is interesting that the statements made and cited above in the Bible, referencing the oneness of God, are translated loosely in the Mormon Church. They interpret these statements not to be literal in nature. However, they do say that in all references to the plurality of God, these statements are to be taken literally. When I say 'plurality', I am meaning the three-ness of God, or the separate and distinct qualities of God, Jesus and the Holy Spirit.

There are many points in the Bible that do not necessarily point to plurality, but 3 persons of God – where they are mentioning Heavenly Father, Jesus and the Holy Spirit. On a personal note, I would argue that all of these citations can be explained through the Trinity. For example, Mormons will site Genesis 1:26, "And God said, let us make man in our image, after our likeness." Within the Mormon Church, the term 'our' is plural and inferred to mean the likeness of Jesus and God, as separate beings. However, if you look back at our example of family, the Father and Jesus are distinct entities with one essence.

The Literal Son of God

In those lines, I would bring your attention to the next verse, Genesis 1:27, "So God created man in his own image." To paraphrase, in these two verses

God is saying that He wanted to create man in their image, so He created them in His image. This to me indicates that 'their' image is 'His' image, therefore they are one and the same. As we said before, it is stated several times within the Bible that all three – God, Jesus and the Holy Spirit – are one. They can manifest independently, act in different ways and be seen throughout the Bible mentioned individually, but that does not disregard or rescind their oneness.

The nature of God in the Mormon Church does not just differ on the point of whether or not God is 'one in three' (Trinity), or three separate entities (Mormon Godhead). The LDS Church also believes in a different nature of God altogether. They suggest that God has a body of flesh and bone. This is contrary to the teachings of mainstream Christianity, which believes per John 4:24 that "God is a Spirit; and they that worship him must worship him in spirit and in truth."

The Bible clearly says here that God is a spirit. But in the Doctrine and Covenants 130:22, "The Father has a body of flesh and bones as tangible as man's; the Son also; but the Holy Ghost has not a body of flesh and bones, but is a personage of Spirit." This is further demonstrated in Doctrine and Covenants 130:1, "When the Savior shall appear we shall see him as he is. We shall see that he is a man like ourselves." It is important to understand that just as we exist in human flesh, Mormons believe that God also exists in flesh. This belief will become increasingly important when we discuss the topics of exaltation and salvation.

Mentioning once more John 14:9, "He that hath seen me hath seen the Father," most Christian churches would interpret this literally. To me, this says that when you look at Jesus, you are looking at God, which is only possible because they are of one essence. However, Mormons actually interpret this to mean the Jesus looks like God.

Since Jesus is considered by Mormons to be the literal Son of God, begotten by God the Father, they believe God is actually Jesus' dad and they should look alike just as we look like our parents. This portion of the Mormon Doctrine counters the teachings of the Bible, saying that Jesus and God are man just like us.

The LDS Church is even confusing in their own doctrine with references between God and Jesus. In Doctrine & Covenants 132:2 they state, "I am the Lord thy God; and I give unto you this commandment – that no man shall come unto the Father but by me or my word, which is my law, saith the Lord." Personally I feel that this statement could only make sense if Mormons believed in the Trinity, which they do not. Put yourself in the mindset of Mormons, saying that Jesus and God are separate individuals.

The Lord thy God would refer to God, right? In their own text, God gives a commandment that 'no man shall come unto the Father but by me'. So, if God is the Father, and he is speaking, how can no one come to God except through God? Unless, of course, when he is saying 'I am the Lord thy God' that he is actually speaking from the perspective of Jesus.

However, if that were the case, why would Jesus call himself God? The only way that this passage within the Mormon's own doctrine would make sense would be if you did believe in the Trinity, because God and Jesus are one and the same.

A Spirit of Guidance & Conscience

The Holy Spirit, within mainstream Christianity, is something that is conferred upon you at baptism. I was baptized into the LDS church at the age of eight. I was told that I was at the age of accountability, and it was time for me to be baptized.

After I was baptized, I sat in a chair. My father and three other elders in the church laid their hands upon my head, and bestowed upon me the gift of the Holy Spirit.

I was told that after baptism I had been cleansed of all of my sins, and they were giving me the gift of the Holy Spirit to help me differentiate right from wrong – after that point, I was responsible for my actions and God would punish me for those actions if I did not repent. In this way, the Holy Ghost was to be my moral compass.

In the Mormon Church, they also believe that when you receive the Holy Spirit, you also receive some manifestations of the spirit – or spiritual talents. "And again, it is given by the Holy Ghost to some to know the diversities of operations, whether they be of God, that the manifestations of the Spirit may be given to every man to profit withal" Doctrine and Covenants 46:16.

A person can receive the word of wisdom, word of knowledge, faith to be healed, faith to heal, working of miracles, prophesy, discerning of spirits, speaking with tongues, and interpretation of tongues. It is the gift of the Bishop of each Mormon Church to discern these gifts and ensure that no one of those gifts is of satanic nature.

Jesus is Less than God

On a personal note, the Trinity has always been one of the most difficult things for me to understand as a person relatively new to mainstream Christianity. It is difficult for any person to fully comprehend, and it is even more difficult for people coming from Mormonism. The nature of God is where it all starts, and where the falsehoods of Mormonism are propagated from. As a child in the Mormon Church, the Godhead is all that I knew.

How could three beings possibly be one being? It is difficult to understand and comprehend that God, Jesus and the Holy Spirit are three in one, and not three separate beings altogether. Within my personal research I have found that the Mormon vantage point on this issue is not indicative of the way that the Bible describes this phenomenon. The Mormon distortion of the nature of God completely alters the importance of Jesus, making him somewhat lesser than God in power.

You may notice that if you have driven by or been inside of a Mormon Church, you never see any crucifixes. There are no crucifixes on the steeples, no crosses on the walls or anywhere on their buildings. Inside of the Churches there are no crosses, only paintings of Jesus.

When I was little I always saw other girls wearing pretty necklaces around their necks with beautiful crosses, and I wanted one too. When I asked my

Sunday school teacher why we don't get to wear a cross, I was told that 'we don't worship the cross.' While I don't share this belief now, it took me until I was much older to put two and two together, and understand why my teacher said this.

What my Sunday school teacher meant was that we worship God, and not exclusively Jesus. Since the Mormon Church believes that God, Jesus and the Holy Spirit are completely separate, they do not want you to worship Jesus exclusively and lose sight of God. The Mormon view on mainstream Christianity is that most Christians worship Jesus and his work on the cross and neglect God.

However, from the perspective of mainstream Christianity and believing in the Trinity and worshipping the sacrifices of Jesus, we are simultaneously worshipping God because they are one and the same. This is an incredibly important distinction in the Nature of God, and how mainstream Christianity differs drastically from the Mormon perspective.

Standing Alone

The Nature of God is fundamental to Christianity, and that is one of the major areas where Mormonism stands alone. Every person is entitled to interpret the scriptures in their own way, but some statements are made many times and are resoundingly clear throughout the Bible. Understanding the very nature of God is a keystone to understanding your own Christianity.

Many Mormons have never been given the opportunity to understand the nature of God any differently than they were told as a child, and it's a very confusing concept to understand the Trinity once those seeds of misunderstanding have been planted.

It can be said that the nature of God and this common belief is what ties all of Christianity together. While all Christian Churches may argue the points of baptism, communion and other acts of faith, we all commonly agree on the nature of God.

There is no true disagreement between Christian Churches of who God is, and the nature of the triune God. When you change the nature of God, you change religions. The Mormon distortion of the nature of God changes the Christian faith entirely, and you will soon see how this changes the views on the most important subjects in the church.

GRACE & ORIGINAL SIN

What is grace? That's a big subject. Again, as I have found so many things to be in the Mormon Church, the Mormon view on grace is similar but different to mainstream Christianity. Grace is a small word with huge implications. The misinterpretation or revision of the meaning of grace can change God's entire plan for all of us – and I have found that in the Mormon Church, it does.

What the heck is Grace?

In mainstream Christianity, we believe in grace. Grace is given by God, and through our faith in God alone we are saved. The principle of grace is that Jesus sacrificed himself and paid for our sins so that we can be saved in the eyes of God. At the end of days when we all stand in judgment before God, the blood and sacrifice of Christ will cover the sins of those who are believers in Him and He will spare us the punishment we deserve as sinners.

Those who did not believe in Him will not be covered by their faith and will be cast into Hell, as punishment for those sins which are so visible and unshielded. Put plainly, if we put our faith in God and believe in Christ, we will be saved. This is so clearly stated in one of my favorite verses, Ephesians 2:4-10. This entire section is imperative to the meaning of grace, and it reads as follows:

"But God, who is rich in mercy, for his great love wherewith he loved us, Even when we were dead in sins, hath quickened us together with Christ, (by grace ye are saved;) And hath raised us up together, and made us sit together in heavenly places in Christ Jesus: That in the ages to come he might shew the exceeding riches of his grace in his kindness toward us through Christ Jesus. *For by grace are ye saved through faith*; and that not of yourselves: *Not of works*, lest any man should boast; For we are his workmanship, created in Christ Jesus unto good works, which God hath before ordained that we should walk in them."

This statement is so abundantly clear to me. Before Christ, we were dead in our sins. Like a blanket of love and faith, the blood of Christ covers us in the eyes of God. Through His sacrifice, our sins are shielded from God's sight, so when He looks upon us He only sees the perfection of Jesus and not the deeds we have done. As believers and followers of Christ, we are given this amazing gift of grace which permits us as unworthy sinners to enter the Kingdom of Heaven. Through faith in Christ, through God's grace, we are saved.

There are no works involved in attaining salvation, but rather good works are the fruit of our relationship with God. This is reiterated in Titus 3:5-6, saying "he saved us, *not because of works done by righteousness*, but according to his own mercy, by the washing of regeneration and renewal of the Holy Spirit, whom he poured out on us richly through Jesus Christ our Savior."

All through my childhood, I had never heard the word grace. I would not say that Mormon Church does not believe in or teach grace on some level, but I would argue that the principles of grace that they perpetuate are not truly grace at all.

Grace + Works = Not Really Grace

Grace within the LDS church is conditional, and as such I would argue that it is not truly grace. As we mentioned earlier in Ephesians 2, we are saved by grace through faith alone. However, in the Book of Mormon 2 Nephi 25:23, grace is given an entirely different meaning, "For we labor diligently to write, to persuade our children and also our brethren, to believe in Christ and to be reconciled to God; for we know that it is by grace that we are saved, *after all we can do.*" Wow. Hold the phone.

Those five words on the end changed the entire grace game completely. After all we can do? That is a clear statement of works – actions and tasks that must be performed. These five words are saying that we must perform good works – and then we are *eligible* to be saved by grace through our faith in God.

This distortion of grace is perpetuated throughout the Book of Mormon, shown again in Mosiah 4:6-8, "I say unto you, if ye have come to a knowledge of the goodness of God, and his matchless power, and his wisdom, and his patience, and his long-suffering towards the children of men, and also, the atonement which has been prepared from the foundation of the world, that thereby salvation might come to him that should put his trust in the Lord, *and should be diligent in keeping his commandments*, and continue in the faith even unto the end of his life, I mean the life of the mortal body – I say that this is the man who receiveth salvation…And there is none other salvation save this which hath been spoken of; neither are there any conditions whereby man can be saved except the conditions which I have told you."

So first, this passage in the Book of Mormon is stating that there are works involved with attaining salvation. Secondly, this passage is stating that it is only through the plan of salvation written in the Book of Mormon alone and therefore *not* that written in the Bible that we are saved.

The Book of Mormon actually goes so far as to mock mainstream Christianity and their view on the Bible, in 2 Nephi 29:3&11, saying, "And because my words shall hiss forth – many of the Gentiles shall say: A Bible! A Bible! We have got a Bible and there cannot be any more Bible…For I command all men, both in the east and in the west, and in the north, and in the south, and in the islands of the sea, that they shall write the words which I speak unto them; for out of the books which shall be written I will *judge the world, every man according to their works,* according to that which is written."

Not only do they mock the belief in the bible being the sole and inerrant Word of God, they also again openly state very clearly their belief in every man being judged by his works. I find it greatly disturbing that such a mockery is made of the Bible in the Book of Mormon. If it is the Word of God as even Mormons believe it to be, it should be revered and not cast down and ridiculed.

You've Gotta Be Good

In our minds it is easy to understand acts. After all, we are taught as a child to be good people, to do good works, and to be kind to others. How can Mother Teresa be on the same level as me, a lowly sinner? How can I be worthy of heaven after all of my sins? Don't I have to do something to be awarded with Heaven? According to Ephesians 2, God says no. You are good enough just as you are, by the grace of God given through his son, Jesus Christ. All you have to do is believe and trust in Him.

However, simple good acts are still not enough in the Mormon faith. If your mother asks you to do something and you do it, is that a good act? Well, the answer would be yes and no.

Truly good acts are those which are performed of your own accord. "Verily I say, men should be anxiously engaged in a good cause, and do many things of their own free will, and bring to pass much righteousness; For the power is in them, wherein they are agents unto themselves. And inasmuch as men do good they shall in nowise lose their reward. But he that doeth not anything until he is commanded, and receiveth a commandment with a doubtful heart, and keepeth it with slothfulness, the same is damned" Doctrine & Covenants 58:27-29.

So for lack of a better term – you're damned if you do and damned if you don't. While it's smiled upon to do good works, the only way you can get real 'credit' for your good actions within the Mormon Church is if they are unprompted good actions done with a willing heart. Not only do you have to do good works, you must do certain types of good works. Where is the grace in that?

You've Gotta Forgive

Further to the good works is the act of forgiveness, which I believe also falls into the category of acts. We all know that we are supposed to forgive each other, as the Bible certainly teaches this. However, there is a slight addition in the Mormon Church which again places consequences on the heads of Mormon followers for not practicing forgiveness. "Verily, verily, I say unto you, my servants, that inasmuch as you have forgiven one another your trespasses, even so I, the Lord, forgive you. Nevertheless, there are those among you who have sinned exceedingly; yea, even all of you have sinned; but verily I say unto you, beware from henceforth, and refrain from sin, lest sore judgments fall upon your heads" Doctrine & Covenants 82:1-2. Not giving forgiveness is considered to be a sin. If you do not forgive, you will not receive forgiveness from God and he will lay judgment upon you for that sin. Where is the grace in that?

You've Gotta Be Good Parents

There is great responsibility placed upon parents in the Mormon Church. All Mormons are encouraged to raise their children strongly in the church. When I was a child, my parents gave me a ring that was silver and green. On it was a shield that said 'CTR'. CTR means 'Choose the Right', and is a phrase to live by as a child in the LDS church. As a child of free will, it was our responsibility to always choose the right.

After all, we are saved by grace plus works, and we must learn to choose the right early in our lives – it was my parent's responsibility to instill that belief in me. "Every spirit of man was innocent in the beginning; and God having redeemed man from the fall, men became again, in their infant state, innocent before God. And that wicked one cometh and taketh away light and truth, through disobedience, from the children of men, and because of the tradition of their fathers. But I have commanded you to bring up your children in light and truth" Doctrine & Covenants 93:38-40. For my parents, ingraining this 'truth' and encouraging us to 'choose the right' was part of their responsibility to God as parents.

Within my life, this was one of the hardest aspects of Mormonism to overcome, and this is why grace is so difficult for ex-Mormons to understand. This is a concept that is pushed onto them as children and it is very difficult to unravel these teachings. How can this life not possibly be about works? How do I not have to always do good deeds to go to heaven? Isn't God keeping a scorecard of my life, and tallying up how many good deeds I have done?

It is so much easier to believe that we have to *do* something to go to heaven. After all, we have to study for tests to make good grades and work late at our jobs to get that promotion – why wouldn't our spiritual responsibilities mirror this concept? Because God says so and because grace is just that – grace.

Love (and Spy On) Thy Neighbors

One of the most comical things for me about Mormonism is that they are called upon by the Church to call each other out on their sins. When I was a baby living in Utah with my parents, my mother would catch fellow church members digging through her trash. It should be noted that this was not an isolated incident – I have known several people in Utah who admitted this happened to them as well. What were they digging for?

Evidence of sin. They wanted to find beer bottles or cigarette butts or coffee grinds or something – anything at all to prove that my parents were guilty of sin. No, they were not targeting my parents in particular.

This was a regular occurrence in Utah, possibly as a result of Doctrine & Covenants 104:10, "And now I give unto you the power from this very hour, that if any man among you, of the order, is found a transgressor and repenteth not of the evil, that ye shall deliver him over unto to buffetings of Satan; and he shall not have power to bring evil upon you."

It is the responsibility of church-goers to find transgressors in their congregation, and if they will not repent for those transgressions, they should be delivered up to Satan. As a result, he won't have any power to bring evil upon you. Pretty good deal for the finder of transgressions, wouldn't you say?

Contradicting Grace in the Bible

Grace within the LDS church undeniably encompasses acts. While they will not deny the Bible or its teachings outright, the Book of Mormon undoubtedly opens this door where grace is no longer grace. It is grace with works. And this open door is what leads to the levels of heaven, as discussed in the next chapter. The Mormon view on grace is the foundation on which the staircase to heaven is built.

In Ephesians 2 it even goes so far as to clearly point out that we are *not* saved by works. We are purposefully not saved by works, so that no man can claim to have lived a more righteous life than another – "Not of works lest any man should boast." But those five little words in the Book of Mormon change the essence of grace entirely, and it simply must be said that the Book of Mormon and the Bible contradict each other here.

Mormons maintain that the Book of Mormon is an additional word of God – it's another scripture, viewed as even more important and correct than the Bible. So let's say that we just run with them on this one and say that the Book of Mormon is another scripture.

If there were another scripture, it could only agree with the information supplied to us by God through His word, right? However, both the New and Old Testaments make specific statements regarding the addition of information to the teachings of the Bible.

This is seen in Deuteronomy 4:2, which says, "Ye shall not add unto the word which I command you, neither shall ye diminish ought from it". And again it is seen in Revelations 22:18-19, which says, "…If any man shall add unto these things, God shall add unto him the plagues that are written in this book: And if any man shall take away from the words of the book of this prophecy, God shall take away his part out of the book of life…"

I will argue full-heartedly that those five words in 2 Nephi 25:23, "…*after all we can do*" are an addition to the Bible. That information was not presented in the Bible. There is no place in the Bible that states grace plus works. That is an addition to the Bible, and as a contradiction to the clear words of the Bible, it simply cannot be true.

Grace is a complicated subject, primarily because it is can so easily be misconstrued. Often people confuse where 'acts' come into play, and are doing good deeds but with the wrong understanding of where those deeds fall in terms of salvation. We do not do good deeds to be saved.

There is no scorecard in Heaven, and while God knows what we are doing at any given moment in our lives, he is not keeping a tally of our wrongdoings and our good deeds to determine where we will sit in Heaven.

We do good works because of God – as a result of our relationship with God – but *not* to earn points with God. This is an incredibly important distinction to make to all Christians, but most importantly to Mormons, who believe their salvation hinges on the balance of good works versus sin.

Original Sin – What's that?

We have clarified grace and the Mormon concept of grace + works, but we have not yet touched on the topic of original sin. The concepts of original sin and grace go hand-in-hand. The reason we need grace is because of our original sin. We are sinful beings by nature, and there is nothing that can be done to help that, right? Mormons say no.

Mainstream Christianity generally identifies that there are two forms of sin, actual sin and original sin. Actual sins are familiar to all of us – they are the sins that we commit daily. Original Sin, however, is the sin of all humanity as a result of the sin of Adam and Eve. The fall of man is the reason we all die – and the reason that Jesus had to die to give us His grace.

Original sin is discussed clearly in Romans 5:12-19, saying, "Wherefore, as by one man sin entered into the world, and death by sin; and so death passed upon all men, for that all have sinned; (For until the law sin was in the world: but sin is not imputed when there is no law. Nevertheless death reigned from Adam to Moses, even over them that had not sinned after the similitude of Adam's transgression, who is the figure of him that was to come…) Therefore as by the offence of one judgment came upon all men to condemnation; even so by the righteousness of one the free gift came upon all men unto justification of life. For as by one man's disobedience many were made sinners, so by the obedience of one shall many be made righteous."

This passage is outstanding at both identifying and describing the nature of original sin. It explains that sin entered the world through one man (original sin), and death entered the world through sin. All people will experience death because all people sin. This passage also says that all must die as a result of the falling of Adam because we are all a part of original sin, but our sins have been paid for by Christ's death.

As Christians we all know that we will face death because of original sin, but we have no fear of death because of God's grace. Adam's disobedience made all men sinners, but Christ's obedience made all men who would believe and trust in Him righteous again in the eyes of God.

Paul makes this clear in Romans 5:12-19, but the Mormon Church acknowledges and then tweaks this. The second article of faith in the Mormon Church, states that "... men will be punished for their own sins, and not for Adam's transgression." They believe that people are accountable for their own actions, and will be judged according to those actions.

This line of thought seems bit slippery for me, because the punishment for Adam's transgression is death. If we all experience death, then we are all subject to the fall of Adam and subsequent original sin. While mainstream Christians will agree that we should certainly avoid sin, they will also agree that grace covers and erases those sins. Yet the question that is still poised in my head is: if we all still die, aren't we all still subject to original sin, just as the Bible says we are?

God & Adam Chat about Baptism

The Mormon belief in punishment for personal sins is traced back to the Book of Mormon, Moses 6:51-68. In these verses, God and Adam are having a little 'Q&A' session.

God Speaking to Adam: "...If thou wilt turn unto me, and harken unto my voice, and believe, and repent of all they transgressions, and be baptized, even in water,... ye shall receive the gift of the Holy Ghost, asking all things in his name, and whatsoever ye shall ask, it shall be given you."

Adam: "…Why is it that men must repent and be baptized in water?"

God: "Behold, I have forgiven thee thy transgression in the Garden of Eden. Hence came the saying abroad among the people that the Son of God hath atoned for original guilt, wherein the sins of the parents cannot be answered upon the heads of the children…it is given unto them to know good from evil; wherefore they are agents unto themselves…"

In these verses, God forgives Adam for the original sin and says that through the death and resurrection of Christ, all people have the ability to choose good or evil and are no longer subject to original sin. The punishment for original sin is death. If we are forgiven for original sin as the Book of Mormon says, then it would follow that we should also not continue to be punished for that forgiven sin. Yet, we still experience death. How can it be that we are forgiven for our sin, yet still punished for it?

The Ability to Choose Right & Wrong

Book of Mormon, Moses 6:51-68 continues:

God: "…I have given unto you another law and commandment. Wherefore teach it unto your children, that all men, everywhere, must repent, or they can in nowise inherit the kingdom of God, for no unclean thing can dwell there, or dwell in his presence…by reason of transgression cometh the fall, which bringeth death, and inasmuch as ye were born into the world by water, and blood, and the spirit, which I have made, and so became of dust a living soul, even so ye must be born again into the kingdom of heaven, of water, and of the Spirit, and be cleansed by blood, even the blood of mine Only Begotten; that ye might be sanctified from all sin, and enjoy the words of eternal life in this world, and eternal life in the world to come, even immortal glory. For by the water ye keep the commandment; by the Spirit ye are justified, and by the blood ye are sanctified."

This verse from Mormon scripture is saying that since you know the difference between good and evil and can make choices based on that knowledge, if you commit and sin and do not repent for it you cannot enter into celestial heaven, which will be explained in detail later. It then reiterates this and adds that you must be baptized, have the Holy Spirit, and repent to enter heaven. Doctrine & Covenants 29:17 takes this even further, saying "And it shall come to pass, because of the wickedness of the world, that I will take vengeance upon the wicked, for they will not repent; for the cup of mine indignation is full; for behold, my blood shall not cleanse them if they hear me not."

In essence, if you are baptized and receive the Holy Spirit, but you refuse to allow the Spirit to guide you in decisions between right and wrong, God will leave you. So despite the grace of God being poured out on you from the sacrifice of Christ, grace is conditional and the blood of Christ will not cover you if you do not also follow these rules.

Even more than God leaving your side, this verse is saying that God will take vengeance upon you because you are wicked and will not repent. This is why Mormons so strongly believe in repentance after every sin – fear of vengeance from God and losing a spot in Heaven.

There are also some people mentioned in the Doctrine & Covenants that are actually exempt from sin. In the history of the Bible, there has only ever been one man exempt from sin. However, the Doctrine & Covenants actually contends that there are men in this world who are considered holy and have no sin, "Wherefore, I will that all men shall repent, for all are under sin, except those which I have reserved unto myself, holy men that ye know not of" Doctrine & Covenants 49:8.

Are there people amongst us who have no sin? Are Mormons contending that there is another Jesus here or to come? Or do they believe that their Prophets are without sin? This verse opens too many questions for me, but I believe that it is important to know this perspective which demonstrates that such perfection as Christ's is attainable.

I am not saying that today, we do not know the difference between good and evil – of course we do. But in Ephesians 2:8 it says, "For by grace are ye saved through faith – and this is not from yourselves." This says nothing of repentance. Grace is a gift from God, whereby we don't have to be perfect people to earn a place with God in heaven. Grace is given, not earned. Should we ask God for forgiveness for our sins? Absolutely. Is it mandatory that we ask forgiveness for every sin before we will go to heaven? Must we be completely sinless before God will open His arms to us? In my opinion, the Bible says no.

Adam & Eve Fell on Purpose

So, if there is no original sin and we are free agents roaming around making our own good and bad choices, what is the point? Mormons believe that Adam's sin was actually necessary to further God's plan of life and Salvation. In essence, God made Adam fall on purpose. Without Adam's sin, we would not have the ability to prove ourselves before God. In the Book of Mormon, 2 Nephi 2:25, it says that "Adam fell that men might be; and men are, that they might have joy." For Mormons, life is viewed as one big test from God. Now *that* is changing the meaning of life.

Perfection is Attainable

We've gone up the stairs where grace is not really grace, and original sin was created on purpose as a test from God. Let's journey up another step on the staircase. By mainstream Christianity standards, we are all inherently sinful. By LDS standards, we are to strive for perfection. Now, I need to be very clear about this idea of perfection. There is a very big difference between striving to do what is right to please the Lord *because* you are Christian, and striving to do what is right and please the Lord to *attain* your salvation. Again, this goes back to the same idea of grace – we strive to be perfect in the eyes of God because of our faith, and not because we are trying to earn points for our salvation.

The Mormon ideal of perfection is illustrated in the Book of Mormon, Moroni 10:32-33, "Yea, come unto Christ and be perfected in him, and deny yourselves of all ungodliness; and if ye shall deny yourselves of all ungodliness, and love God with all your might, mind and strength, then is his grace sufficient for you, that by his grace ye may be perfect in Christ; and if by the grace of God ye are perfect in Christ, ye can nowise deny the power of God. And again, if ye by the grace of God are perfect in Christ, and deny not his power, then are ye sanctified in Christ by the grace of God, through the shedding of the blood of Christ, which is in the covenant of the Father unto the remission of your sins, that ye become holy, without spot." These verses tell people of the Mormon faith that they must deny themselves of ungodliness – strive for perfection – to receive God's grace. This standard of perfection for the receipt of grace was one of the reasons I fell out of the Mormon faith. It is impossible for a person to be perfect, even if we make perfection the constant focus of our thoughts.

One thing that is absolutely guaranteed is that no matter how hard you try, no matter how many good deeds you perform or how much money you give to charities or how often you do the right thing, you will never, ever be perfect. You can strive for it, but you will always fail. There was only ever one perfect being, and it isn't you. So throughout my childhood in the church, I always had awareness that I was a failure at my faith, and I was never good enough for God's grace.

Of course, it is recognized by Mormons that perfection is difficult, and that is why their church also promotes the ideals of repentance. Alma 42:22-25, "But there is law given, and a punishment affixed, and a repentance granted, which repentance, mercy claimeth; otherwise, justice claimeth the creature and executeth the law, and the law inflicteth the punishment; if not so, the works of justice would be destroyed, and God would cease to be God. But God ceaseth not to be God, and mercy claimeth the penitent, and mercy cometh because of the atonement; and the atonement bringeth to pass the resurrection of the dead; and the resurrection of the dead bringeth back men into the presence of God; and thus they are restored into his presence, to be judged according to their works, according to the law and justice. For behold, justice exerciseth all his demands, and also mercy claimeth all which is her own; and thus, *none but the truly penitent are saved.*"

Again, wow. Hold the phone one more time. Grace is now not only granted 'after all we can do', but it is now also subject to the repentance of the sinner. The basic message is, don't commit any sins, and if you do, you had better repent for them or suffer the consequences of an eternity in hell.

This word is continued further and in more clarity in Alma 42:27-29, "Therefore, O my son, whosoever will come may come and partake of the waters of life freely; and whosoever will not come the same is not compelled to come; but in the last day it shall be restored unto him according to his deeds. If he has desired to do evil, and has not repented of his days, behold, evil shall be done unto him, according to the restoration of God. And now, my son, I desire that ye should let these things trouble you no more, and only let your sins trouble you, with that trouble which shall bring you down unto repentance."

To me, this particular verse provides the connection between faith, works, repentance and salvation – and demonstrates how all of these pieces fit together and are dependent upon each other in the Mormon faith. It also clearly states that God has "given unto you another law and commandment".

However, reflecting back upon Deuteronomy 4:2 and Revelations 22:18-19, I will repeat that we cannot add to the teachings of the Bible. By mandating repentance (a work) to enter the kingdom of heaven, that is an addition to the teachings of the Bible where again, it states that we are saved by grace through faith and not by any action of our own.

Grace is a magnificent gift. I did not learn about grace until my adult life, most likely because our view of grace when I was growing up in the LDS Church was not truly grace at all. Receiving grace in the Mormon faith is a multi-step process.

First step: the Mormon faith believes in grace after all you can do, which is a statement of required works. Second step: they do not believe in original sin, but rather that people must repent for their own individual sins before receiving grace. Third step: you must be baptized to receive grace.

I believe that it is absolutely imperative that Christians understand the meaning of grace, and what the Bible specifically states about it. When we lose sight of grace and what that really means, then we lose sight of the importance of the gift of Christ. I also think that it is important to acknowledge the fact that within the Mormon Church, the only references to grace made also tie in many other facets that were not in the Bible. To me, this is adding to the Bible, which the Bible itself says is unacceptable.

Personally, I am incredibly grateful for grace. It took me so many years to really understand what grace means to me, and to my relationship with God. We are not perfect people, and this constant striving for an unattainable level of perfection only ever put a strain on my relationship with God. Now I understand that it is through my relationship with God alone that I receive His grace, and *that* is a magnificent thing to be grateful for.

Revelations & Prophecy

As it is made evident by the doctrine of the Mormon Church that revelations and prophecies are the cornerstone of their belief. Without belief in revelations and prophecies, the Book of Mormon, Doctrine & Covenants, and Pearl of Great Price would not exist. They were and still are, after all, created entirely based on the revelations by Prophets of the Mormon Church.

In fact, the entire foundation of the Mormon Church, as you read from the historical portion of this book, is based upon Joseph Smith's encounters with God. There is much debate within Christianity regarding whether or not visions, or revelations, indeed exist in modern-day Christianity.

I will not dispute whether or not someone personally experiences God or something God-like through revelations or visions. It is not my place to make the assumption that these gifts do not exist. However, I can explain the fundamentals of revelations in the Mormon Church and how they shape the actions of its followers.

I can also provide some citations from the Bible which will challenge certain principles within the Mormon Church that are a result of those revelations. There are several interesting places in the Bible where it does not necessarily speak to the physicality of revelations, but it does speak to the addition of doctrines and teaching as well as what doctrine we are expected to follow.

Living Prophets

The Mormon faith believes that revelations exist. They existed in the past, and they still exist today. In fact, four of the thirteen Articles of Faith in the Mormon Church are dedicated to revelations and prophecies. The Merriam-Webster dictionary defines revelations as "an act of revealing or communicating divine truth" or "something that is revealed by God to humans." They define prophecies as "an inspired utterance of a prophet" or "a prediction of something to come." The fifth Article of Faith states that a "Man must be called of God, by prophecy, and by the laying on of hands by those who are in authority, to preach the Gospel and administer in the ordinances thereof."

This is saying that all people are called to their offices within the church – all the way down to the librarian and the nursery leader – by prophecy. They are in those positions because they were prophesized to take on that role. In my experience with the Mormon Church, I had never seen someone be called by prophecy to perform a role in the church and deny or refuse to take on the role that was requested of them.

The sixth Article of Faith in the Mormon Church states that they "believe in the same organization that existed in the Primitive Church, namely apostles, prophets, pastors, teachers, evangelists and so forth." It is fundamental to the Mormon Church that they believe in Prophets, and they believe that the President of the Mormon Church is a living prophet. In this way, the leader of the Mormon Church is viewed to be much like Peter or any of the other Apostles who revealed truths in the Bible.

This belief also enables the living prophet to change, modify and alter their doctrine to accommodate for details they believe are missing or incorrect, and adjust their doctrine to keep up with present-day issues. It is the belief in those living prophets, including Joseph Smith, which led to the establishment of the modern-day Mormon Church and the creation of the Doctrine & Covenants and the Pearl of Great Price – both doctrines founded on prophecy and revelations.

The seventh Article of Faith takes this further, saying they "believe in the gift of tongues, prophecy, revelation, visions, healing, interpretation of tongues, and so forth." This article states outright the belief in prophecy, revelations and visions, as well as speaking in tongues. Speaking in tongues is defined in Merriam Webster as "a charisma identified by ecstatic usually unintelligible speech." While my personal experience in the Mormon Church never involved witnessing people speaking in tongues, it is still a gift that few may possess and is still a permissible concept in mainstream Christianity today.

The last Article of Faith related to prophecy and revelation is the ninth article, stating "We believe all that God has revealed, all that He does now reveal, and we believe that He will yet reveal many great and important things pertaining to the Kingdom of God." This articulates their belief both in the past, present and future revelations. They believe in all that Joseph Smith and the Mormon Prophets have revealed, all that the current living prophet is revealing now, and they are determined to believe all that future prophets of the Mormon faith will prophesize.

Biblical Warnings

It should be noted that there are several places in the Bible where there are warnings and foresight, saying clearly that we should never stray from those words written in the Bible. Straying from the original intent of the Bible is a most serious offense, and leads to great confusion amongst all Christians.

In 2 Thessalonians 2:15 it states, "Therefore, brethren, stand fast, and hold the traditions which ye have been taught, whether by word, or our epistle." There is no mention in this text of holding on to any word other than the Bible. This is reiterated in 1 Peter 1:25, "But the word of the Lord endureth forever. And this is the word which by the gospel is preached unto you." The word of God is finite and is taught within the words of the Bible.

And yet again this is shown in Joshua 23:6, "Be ye therefore very courageous to keep and do all that is written in the book of the law of Moses, that yet shall not turn aside therefrom to the right hand or to the left," saying that we must do all that is said in the bible, and never turn away from it.

It is interesting to note that there are several passages, these three included, where we are given specific instructions not to turn away from the Bible in any way. This would seemingly include turning away from the Bible to turn towards another scripture.

Open to Interpretation

The Mormon argument is that they do not disagree with the Bible, only that they believe that the Book of Mormon is more correct. Believing in the Prophet and the Book of Mormon is an act of faith, and they are called to look to their hearts for the answers from God. You cannot argue that Mormons do not believe in the Bible, because that is not entirely true.

Mormons support specifically the King James Version of the Bible. As mentioned before, their contention with the Bible is actually that through translation and time it has been changed into a document that was not the original intention of God, and that many of the ordinances of Salvation were lost.

Since Mormons maintain that the original integrity of the Bible was lost due to translation, I feel that there is something to be said here about pastoral training. In my opinion, if you are going to make a serious accusation about the intent and truthfulness of the Bible, you must first have the education and understanding of Biblical languages to translate the ancient transcriptions yourself.

Coming from the Mormon faith I can attest to the fact that very few Mormon leaders know Biblical languages or can translate the original texts of the Bible. It was not until I reached college that I ever heard a person relate Biblical texts back to the original Hebrew and Greek translations. Within most denominations of Christianity there are education requirements for the pastoral leaders of the church, including extensive training in biblical languages and the ability to both read and write in those languages.

This is not the case in the Mormon Church, where bishop leaders are not required to undergo formal higher-level education to attain their position. To that end, I would say that Mormon leaders cannot argue that the intent of the Bible was altered if they cannot read and interpret the original transcriptions of the Bible themselves.

That being said, Mormons offer the Book of Mormon, the Pearl of Great Price and the Doctrine & Covenants to replace the many lost covenants that they maintain should have been part of, or were the original intentions of, the Bible. Of course, since there is no Biblical sanction of these additional teachings, those doctrines were established as a result of divine revelations.

Beyond just the translation of the Bible, Mormons believe that the King James Version of the Bible is the most correct. This is most likely because when they created the King James Version of the Bible, they translated the oldest Biblical transcripts they could find into Old English, the language of the time. There was a system set out to check and double check the transcription work done by those transcribing the pages, and at the time this version was written it was widely accepted to be an accurate translation.

Mormons will also not accept any modern English version to be used in their church, as they again say that there are faults due to interpretation. On that token, I would also personally argue that while some verses may be translated differently than others dependent upon the language, or even the audience (old English versus modern day English), there is little left to the interpretation of man.

Since I have been using the King James Version of the Bible for my studies – to speak apples to apples with the Mormon faith – and found that there is little difference between Bibles other than diction. In fact, many Bibles (NIV included) offer multiple translations noted within the text. For example, when 'and' is written, they denote that 'or' could also be a proper translation from the original text.

The simple fact is that there are some words in the original Hebrew, Aramaic and Greek texts of the Bible which simply do not have direct translations into English or other languages. For that reason, many mainstream Christian Pastors are educated in reading these original texts, to better understand the fundamental meanings of the Bible and the original intentions of those words.

By not accepting the words in the Bible to be the purposeful intent of God, the door becomes open for revelations by man to fill in the gaps – and that can be a very dangerous game to play with the words of God.

Is the Bible the Final Word of God?

As a Christian, it is important to understand the Bible's finality. The Mormon Church does not believe that the words of the Bible are final, but rather just one part in a progressive series of revelations by God of His plans for us. Is it the final word of God? Can you dispute anything it says?

One verse relating to the topic of finality that stood out to me was 1 Timothy 6:14, saying "that thou keep this commandment without spot, unrebukeable, *until the appearing of our Lord Jesus Christ.*" In my interpretation and the interpretation of many mainstream churches, this is a strong statement that we must keep to the word of the Bible without change, as the Bible cannot be altered or argued.

Furthermore, it goes on to state that it must remain unchallenged "until the appearing of our Lord Jesus Christ", also commonly referred to as the Second Coming of Jesus. Many Christian Churches will maintain that this indicates that all revelations related to the change and addition of principles to the Bible has been ceased until the Second Coming.

So what does this verse really mean to us as Christians? If 1 Timothy 6:14 is correct, then God is telling us to keep to the words of the Bible until the Second Coming of Christ, period. There is no reference to another scripture, or any other teachings that he wants us to focus on. Our focus, per his own command, is to be on the Bible and nowhere else.

There are several verses that are quite strong on this subject, even going so far as calling those who would change the Bible in any way to be evil. In Timothy 6:3-5 it says, "If any man teach otherwise, and consent not to wholesome words, even the words of our Lord Jesus Christ, and to the doctrine which is according to godliness, he is proud, knowing nothing, but doting about questions and strifes of words, whereof cometh envy, strife, railings, and evil surmising. Perverse disputings of men of corrupt minds, and destitute of the truth, supposing that gain is godliness; from such withdraw thyself."

This passage is very clear. If any person pulls away from the truth of the Bible and into their own truth, it is an act of conceit, believing that they know more than God. Gain is not Godliness, or knowing more does not afford you any greater righteousness before God.

It also specifically says that this person is 'doting about questions and strifes of words', meaning that they are trying to simply argue about the Bibles content and wording, which will result in 'perverse disputings'. God is saying that some people will argue over words, but since they are His words, there is nothing to argue.

The Mormon belief that the Bible's words were changed over time, in my opinion, is a direct example of this verse. The Mormons challenge the content of the Bible by questioning wording and content, yet their questioning of the contents in the Bible is precisely what pulls people away from God. This is reemphasized in Romans 16:17, saying, "Now I beseech you, brethren, mark them which cause divisions and offences contrary to the doctrine which ye have learned, and avoid them." This is again saying to avoid those who seek to create divisions in the Christian communities.

Yet Mormons continue to argue that their doctrines are not contradicting the beliefs set forth in the Bible. Instead, they would say that there are things missing from the Bible, which they account for.

To that argument I would cite again Deuteronomy 4:2, which says, "Ye shall not add unto the word which I command you, neither shall ye diminish ought from it, that ye may keep the commandments of the Lord your God which I command you." In this verse it is made abundantly clear that we cannot take anything away, *nor add anything to*, the Bible.

This is again mentioned very strongly in Revelations 22:18-19 as a warning to those who would add to the Bible, "For I testify unto every man that heareth the words of the prophecy in this book, If any man shall add unto these things, God shall add unto him the plagues that are written in this book: And if any man shall take away from the words of the book of this prophecy, God shall take away his part out of the book of life, and out of the holy city, and from the things which are written in this book." God has made it abundantly clear that any addition or removal from the Bible brings great judgment upon those who would change it.

While Mormons will argue that their view does not depart from the original intent of the Bible, I would disagree on this point. Without particularly the Doctrine & Covenants and the Pearl of Great Price and the revelations which brought those books to existence, Salvation and the Nature of God would have a much different meaning. In fact, I would contend that through revelations and the addition of three entire books of scripture, the Mormon prophets have undoubtedly created additions to the Bible which have altered the Mormon views on those subjects entirely.

Changing, altering and adding to the contents of the Bible will have huge implications on Christianity. There are several warnings offered throughout the Bible, actually foreshadowing and detailing this type of diversion from what most Christians would view to be the truth.

Paul provides a warning in Acts 20:29-30, saying, "For I know this, that after my departing shall grievous wolves enter in among you, not sparing the flock. Also of your own selves men shall arise, speaking perverse things, to draw away disciples after them." Paul is telling us here that once he is gone, there will be people who will say and do things to make you wish to follow in their actions.

There is also very specific reference in the Bible to a falling away from the Gospel that almost foreshadows the establishment of churches such as the Mormon Church. In Galatians 1:6-9, Paul is speaking to the Church and says, "I marvel that ye are so soon removed from him that called you into the grace of Christ unto another gospel: which is not another; but there be some that trouble you, and would pervert the gospel of Christ. But through we, *or an angel from heaven*, preach any other gospel unto you than that which we have preached unto you, let him be accursed."

This particular verse to me is haunting in that it almost calls out the descent of the Angel Moroni to Joseph Smith for the establishment of the Book of Mormon, a new gospel. In Galatians it is specifically stated that not even if an angel came from heaven and told you to preach another gospel, should you turn away from the Bible and its principles. Yet, that is the foundation of Mormonism.

Is your Revelation from God?

One of the most interesting 'revelations about revelations' is presented in Doctrine & Covenants 129:1-9, where Joseph Smith reveals information to church members about false revelations and prophecy, and how to know whether or not a revelation is actually from God. "There are two kinds of beings in heaven, namely: Angels, who are resurrected personages, having bodies of flesh and bones – For instance, Jesus said: Handle me and see, for a spirit hath not flesh and bones, as ye see me have. Secondly: the spirits of just men made perfect, they who are not resurrected, but inherit the same glory. When a messenger comes saying he has a message from God, offer him your hand and request him to shake hands with you. If he be an angel he will do so, and you will feel his hand. If he be the spirit of a just man made perfect he will come in his glory; for that is the only way he can appear – ask him to shake hands with you, but he will not move, because it is contrary to the order of heaven for a just man to deceive; but he will still deliver his message. If it be the devil as an angel of light, when you ask him to shake his hands he will offer you his hand, and you will not feel anything; you may therefore detect him. These are three grand keys whereby you may know whether any administration is from God."

The first time I read this, I had no idea what to think of this verse. Is there actually a code of angelic behavior? A secret handshake? I had heard people joke about Mormons having secret codes, but I had never known this to be true. And yet here it was in writing. Is there a way you can tell that a message is from God? How do we know that the message that told us about the three keys is actually from God to begin with?

The only way you can believe this statement is if you have faith in the doctrine of the Mormon Church and their revelations. Personally, I am reserving my faith for the Bible alone – since God does not address any 'keys' regarding divine revelation in the Bible, I cannot agree that there are keys of revelation at all.

"God said to be Nice to Me"

I also found it very interesting that Joseph Smith had many revelations to his own benefit, rather than the prosperity of the Church. In fact, many of the revelations Joseph Smith had were very short and actually had little to do with religious doctrine.

They had to do with missionary work, appointing positions in the Church, and how members should behave. In Doctrine & Covenants 43:12-13, it was revealed to Joseph Smith that he should tell the members of the Church to provide him with anything he needs while he is translating the Book of Mormon, saying "And if ye desire the glories of the kingdom, appoint ye my servant Joseph Smith, and uphold him before me by the prayer of faith. And again, I say unto you, that if ye desire the mysteries of the kingdom, provide for him food and raiment, and whatsoever thing he needeth to accomplish the work wherewith I have commanded him."

God Messed Up, So We Fixed It

Despite providing him with everything he needed to proceed with translations and revelations, Joseph Smith's words were still admittedly subject to imperfection. The Bible is at no time (within the context of the Bible itself) said to have error. In fact, it is considered to be the opposite – the inerrant word of God. If God wrote the Bible, it is inerrant. Wouldn't it also hold true that all Mormon texts should be considered to be inerrant?

If those of the Mormon faith hold so steady to the concept that the Book of Mormon is truer than the Bible and the Bible contains errors related to our salvation, than it could only be assumed that the Book of Mormon is completely without error, right? It is fascinating to me that this does not hold true.

In fact, the Mormon Church openly states within their texts that they are subject to error as made by man. Doctrine & Covenants 67:4-5 states, "And now I, the Lord, give unto you a testimony of the truth of these commandments which are lying before you. Your eyes have been upon my servant Joseph Smith and his language you have known, and his imperfections you have known; and you have sought in your hearts knowledge that you might express beyond his language; this you also know."

This same sentiment is repeated in the Book of Mormon, 1 Nephi 19:6, saying, "Nevertheless, I do not write anything upon plates save it be that I think it be sacred. And now, if I do err, even did they err of old; not that I would excuse myself because of other men, but because of the weakness which is in me, according to the flesh, I would excuse myself."

The Bible is the inerrant word of God, yet Mormons point their fingers at the Bible and claim it to be so subject to human error that it has lost its integrity. It is ironic that their own doctrine admits to being subject to human error, yet they consider it to be divine and inerrant. I have yet to wrap my mind around that logic.

The permission of revelations in the Mormon Church have allowed for the addition of three additional doctrines, which have changed the original intent of the Bible. I find it interesting and contradictory that Mormons believe that the Bible contains errors, but their texts are error free – when the Bible does not claim to contain any errors but both the Doctrine & Covenants and the Book of Mormon do.

If the Bible is the divine Word of God, written by God, and the Book of Mormon and Doctrine & Covenants are the Word of God through revelation, written by man – wouldn't it be safer to assume that the Bible is the most correct of these scriptures?

SALVATION

Salvation is a very interesting subject in the Mormon Church, as their beliefs on this subject are extremely unique. Salvation is the root of Christianity. We all want to know what is supposed to happen on the other side. However, to understand why the principles of morality are so strongly displayed in the Mormon Church, we must first understand their seed of salvation.

The Spirit World: A Pre-Mortal Life

Mormons believe in a pre-mortal life, which is where they existed before coming to Earth. During our pre-mortal life we live with God the Father as his literal children, resembling him and his image just as Jesus resembled God (again, two separate beings). They believe the God possesses a body of both spirit and flesh, while our pre-mortal bodies are simply spirits.

This is stated in their Doctrine and Covenants 130:22, "The Father has a body of flesh and bones as tangible as man's; the Son also; but the Holy Ghost has not a body of flesh and bones, but is a personage of Spirit. Were it not so, the Holy Ghost could not dwell in us." Although we seemingly exist as spirits and are content in this spirit world, our spirits required more challenge to progress to our potential – introducing an Earthly life.

They believe that God introduces challenges and adversity into our lives, providing us with opportunities to demonstrate our faith, obedience and charity. In essence, we must come to Earth to prove our worthiness to God.

This is further shown in the Pearl of Great Price, Abraham 3: 22-27, "And there stood one among them that was like unto God, and he said unto those who were with him: We will go down, for there is space there, and we will take of these materials, and we will make an earth whereon these may dwell. And we will prove them herewith, to see if they will do all things whatsoever the Lord their God shall command them; And they who keep their first estate shall be added upon; and they who keep not their first estate shall not have glory in the same kingdom with those who keep their first estate; and they who keep their second estate shall have glory added upon their heads forever and ever." This again goes back to Mormons believing that this life is not a gift, but rather a test from God.

Jesus Volunteered to Die

Now, here is where the story is a bit complicated, and perhaps it further explains a bit of how the Mormon Church can believe in the Godhead and not the Trinity.

Mormons believe that the Savior for humankind would have to come to Earth, live a perfect life, take all of the sins of mankind upon him, and then die as a sacrifice for those sins. This is not unlike the belief in mainstream Christianity, but how they come to this conclusion is different. Mormons believe that two of God's spirit children (some may call them angels) volunteered for this task. Lucifer was one of the children, and Jehovah was the other.

This is shown in Moses 4:1-2, "And I, the Lord God, spake unto Moses, saying: That Satan, whom thou hast commanded in the name of mine Only Begotten, is the same which was from the beginning, and he came before me, saying—Behold, here am I, send me, I will be thy son, and I will redeem all mankind, that one soul shall not be lost, and surely I will do it; wherefore give me thine honor. But, behold, my Beloved Son was my Beloved and Chosen from the beginning, said unto me – Father, thy will be done, and the glory be thine forever."

Lucifer wanted to volunteer for this position, but also wanted all of the subsequent glory to be his own. He also wanted to be able to force mankind to do everything he required to regain entry into Heaven. Jehovah, or Jesus, was selected for this task, because he was not seeking glory or domination over mankind.

Often the Mormon Church will use the term 'perdition', or 'sons of perdition'. These are the people who fell from the grace of God, recorded as a revelation in Doctrine & Covenants 76:25-29, "And this we saw also, and bear record, that an angel of God who was in authority in the presence of God, who rebelled against the Only Begotten Son whom the Father loved and who was in the bosom of the Father, was thrust down from the presence of God and the Son, And was called Perdition, for the heavens wept over him – he was Lucifer, a son of the morning. And we beheld, and lo, he is fallen! Is fallen, even a son of the morning! And while we were yet in the Spirit, the Lord commanded us that we should write the vision; for we beheld Satan, that old serpent, even the devil, who rebelled against God, and sought to take the kingdom of our God and his Christ – Wherefore he maketh war with the saints of God, and encompasseth them round about."

Adam Fell on Purpose

Adam and Eve is a classic story, from which Mormons offer little deviation. Adam and Eve lived in the Garden of Eden, where under the commandments of God they were to multiply and replenish the Earth. They were to eat the fruit of any tree they wished, except for the tree of knowledge of good and evil. Lucifer, known as Satan, at this point is a spirit which has been expelled from Heaven. It is Satan who temps Eve to partake in the forbidden fruit.

It mainstream Christianity, Adam's sin was considered a great sin, original sin. Death was not God's intention for men; it was not the way that life was supposed to be. However, Mormons have a different view on the fall of Adam. To align the fall of Adam with their belief in this life as a test, they actually believe that Adam's fall was planned by God and it was God's plan for the progression of humankind.

While they were banished from the Garden of Eden, they now also became subject to death. Mormons believe that God appoints a time for each person to enter what Mormons consider a mortal life. We receive bodies along with families and friends who will support us during our time on Earth. Our time on Earth is crucial, as it is a time in which we must prove ourselves to God. We have complete autonomy, allowing us to choose between good and evil.

God was Jesus' daddy. Literally.

To complicate the story a bit more, we introduce Jesus from the Mormon perspective. Jesus Christ was born to a mortal mother, Mary, and to God, his literal Father. That's correct, his *literal* Father. Doctrine & Covenants 93:21 says, "And now, verily I say unto you, I was in the beginning with the Father, and am the Firstborn."

They believe that just as you may be the firstborn in your family, Jesus was also the firstborn child of God. There is no triune God here where Jesus is God, but rather a Father-Son relationship where Jesus is the literal Son of God. This alters the importance of Jesus, making him lesser than God himself.

Again, this is the same reason that you will not see crucifixes in the Mormon Church, but rather just paintings of Jesus. By worshipping Jesus, they do not believe you are worshipping God, but rather simply a child of God. Since Mormons consider us all considered to be literal children God, this makes all of us equal in some sense to Jesus. This thought process will enable the additional doctrine of levels of heaven, which will be explained later in this chapter.

More Good Acts

It is difficult for many people to stand up to Mormons in terms of faith, because Mormons are certainly some of the nicest, most faithful and most generous people I have ever met. They have a wonderful system of values, and their hearts are rooted in charity. Without question, Mormons are good people with solid moral standing. However, to understand Mormonism it is imperative that you take a closer look at *why* they behave this way.

Mormons believe that no unclean person can return to Heaven. Perfection is their goal, but they recognize that it is an extremely difficult one. Since being perfect in words and actions is a constant challenge, it is nearly impossible to be spotless. We can, however, repent for our sins.

Basically, I would relate this to God keeping a scorecard. You commit a sin, you're at -1. You repent, you're back at zero. You sin twice, you're at -2. You have to repent for both of those sins to get back to zero. They do believe that Jesus was sent to Earth to die and pay the price for our sins, but again, not for grace as we know it. "Therefore I command you to repent – repent, lest I smite you by the rod of my mouth, and by my wrath, and by my anger, and your sufferings be sore – how sore you know not, how exquisite you know not, yea, how hard to bear you know not. For behold, I, God, have suffered these things for all, that they might not suffer *if they would repent*" Doctrine & Covenants 19:15-16.

In the Mormon Church, the grace offered by Christ is simply giving us the opportunity to repent for our sins, be baptized, and then be judged according to our works and whether or not we repented for our sins. The penalty for our sins is the eternal separation from God, and only through Jesus, works and repentance can the hope of returning to God be restored. However, there is no true grace offered in this restoration to God – only the hope of returning to God in some capacity.

Personally, this was one of the most difficult aspects of being a Mormon – constant recognition of bad actions and choices, and no grace in exchange for my faith. When I became a Christian, this was one of the hardest ideals to overcome. Grace is linked directly to original sin, which in turn provides the true plan for salvation. We do not perform good acts to gain entrance into heaven. We do good acts as a result of our relationship with God. This is an incredibly important distinction to make, and again leads to levels of heaven.

You're Dead. Now Make your Choice.

Death is the next step in the staircase of Mormon salvation. In the Mormon Church, death is viewed as one's return to the spirit world. This world is especially important to Mormons because it is the place where those who may not have had the opportunity on Earth to hear God's word can be taught by those who did. Spirits can then choose whether or not to accept God. This leads into Baptisms for the Dead, which I will discuss later in this book.

Mormons believe that the spirits on Earth and in Heaven will continue to bring people to God until the Second Coming of Christ. Upon the Second Coming, faithful spirits will be reunited with their bodies in a resurrection. Mormons believe that when this occurs, God will reign the Earth and Satan will be powerless for one thousand years.

Once the thousand years ends, those who chose to follow Satan will also join their bodies in a second stage of the resurrection. "And again, verily, verily, I say unto you that when the thousand years are ended, and men again begin to deny their God, then will I spare the earth but for a little season; and the end shall come, and the heaven and the earth shall be consumed and pass away, and there shall be a new heaven and a new earth…Michael, mine archangel, shall sound his trump and then shall all the dead awake, for their graves shall be opened, and they shall come forth – yea even all. And the righteous shall be gathered at my right hand unto eternal life; and the wicked on my left hand will I be ashamed to own before the Father. " Doctrine & Covenants 29:22-27.

Mormons believe that all who have lived upon the Earth, good or evil, will receive a physical resurrection as gift from Christ. That is the Mormon sense of grace. However, true salvation from spiritual death – eternal separation from God – is based upon the faith and works of each individual.

Again, the third Article of Faith states, "We believe that through the Atonement of Christ, all mankind may be saved, by <u>obedience</u> to the laws and ordinances of the Gospel." Without obedience and good works, those people will be called wicked and cast into hell.

Three Levels of Heaven

As Christians, we believe, understand and accept that there will be a Judgment Day. This will be the day that we all stand before God, accountable for our actions. However, I must be very careful when I say that we are 'accountable for our actions' and preface that statement by saying that this is where grace fits into Christianity. We are inherently sinful beings. Christ came to the earth to die for our sins, and the reason for such a brutal and vicious death was the depth and depravity of our sinfulness. But Christ died so that we may live again.

As believers and followers of Christ (and therefore God, as they are one and the same), His grace will cover us during Judgment Day. Rather than seeing the depravity of our sins, God will only see the perfection of Christ in us and we will be His, standing under the mercy and grace of Christ given to us through His death on the cross. That is true mercy, and that is true grace. But that is not the belief of the Mormon Church.

A continuation of the debate between Mormons and other members of the Christian community is what Mormons consider to be this final stage of Salvation. Mormons believe that on Judgment Day, souls are separated into three kingdoms of Heaven. Side by side, God the Father and Jesus Christ (as two separate beings) will judge these people based upon their actions in their mortal life. Upon judgment, we will be sent to one of three kingdoms.

- Celestial
- Terrestrial
- Telestial

The Celestial kingdom is the highest of all kingdoms, where we can live eternally with our families, God and Jesus. This kingdom is the permanent residence of God and Jesus (again, two separate individuals). The tenth Article of Faith reads, "We believe in the literal gathering of Israel and in the restoration of the Ten Tribes; that Zion (the New Jerusalem) will be built upon the American continent; that Christ will reign personally upon the earth; and, that the earth will be renewed and receive its paradisiacal glory."

Within the Celestial kingdom, earthly husbands and wives may have Celestial companionship, where they can have spirit children and create worlds of their own where they can enjoy the state of being Gods and Goddesses. This is known as exaltation, and is the ultimate goal in Salvation within the Mormon Church.

Now, this belief in creating their own worlds just as they believe that Jesus created the world is very controversial, even within Mormonism. Most Mormons will say that they certainly do not believe that they can create their own worlds. I know that when I was a practicing Mormon, people asked me about this and a vehemently denied it. However, upon further review of Mormon doctrine, I believe that this is actually true based on their revelations written in the Doctrine & Covenants.

Doctrine & Covenants 132:19-20 states, "And again, verily I say unto you, if a man marry a wife by my word, which is my law, and by the new and everlasting covenant, and it is sealed unto them by the Holy Spirit of promise, by him who is anointed, unto whom I have appointed this power and the keys of this priesthood; and it shall be said unto them – Ye shall come forth in the first resurrection; and if it be after the first resurrection, in the next resurrection; and shall inherit thrones, kingdoms, principalities and powers, dominions, all heights and depths – then shall it be written in the Lamb's Book of Life, that he shall commit no murder whereby to shed innocent blood, and if ye abide in my covenant, and commit no murder whereby to shed innocent blood, it shall be done unto them in all things whatsoever my servant hath put upon them, in time, and through all eternity; and shall be of full force when they are out of the world; and they shall pass by the angels, and the gods, which are set there, to their exaltation and glory in all things, as hath been sealed upon their heads, which glory shall be a fullness and continuation of the seeds forever and ever. *Then they shall be gods, because they have no end; therefore they shall be from everlasting to everlasting, because they continue; then shall they be above all, because all things are subject unto them. Then shall they be gods because they have all power, and the angels are subject unto them.*"

I included this entire verse because I believe it is incredibly important and telling as to why Mormons are so absolute and held by their religious convictions. Furthermore, I believe that this is a complete addition to the Bible, as nowhere in the Bible is there any indication that 1) there are any levels within Heaven and 2) there is any way directly or indirectly for people to become Gods or possess God-like powers.

Yep, you too can be God

This God-like state is directed towards the men of the church who carry the Melchizedek Priesthood, as found in the Church Hierarchy chapter of this book. Upon receiving the Melchizedek priesthood, these priesthood holders believe that they become the Son of God, just as Jesus is the Son of God. "And are priests of the Most High, after the order of Melchizedek, which was after the order of Enoch, which was after the order of the Only Begotten Son. *Wherefore, as it is written, they are gods, even as the sons of God – Wherefore, all things are theirs, whether life or death, or things present, or things to come, all are theirs and they are Christ's, as Christ is God's"* Doctrine & Covenants 76:57-59.

To me, these verses have several meanings. First, it again emphasizes the separateness of Christ and God as two individual people. If Christ can be exalted and worshipped, Mormons equate the people holding the Melchizedek priesthood to be in the same realm as Christ himself. As it says, priesthood holders belong to Christ as Christ belongs to God. Furthermore, this section also speaks to the ability of men in the church to not just become like God – but again to actually be Gods.

This is further reiterated in Doctrine & Covenants 52:13, "And behold, he that is faithful shall be made *ruler over many things*", and yet again in Doctrine & Covenants 88:107, "And then shall the angels be crowned with the glory of His might, and the saints shall be filled with His glory, and receive their inheritance and *be made equal with Him.*"

The verse from Doctrine & Covenants Chapter 88 is clear. The Mormon scriptures do not simply state that the Mormon people strive to become Gods of sorts, perhaps lower than our God. In fact, they state quite clearly that they are to be "equal with Him" and have the power to rule over many things.

If I do everything I am told and play by the Mormon rulebook, I get to become a God in my afterlife? Who wouldn't want to sign up for that deal! But unfortunately the Bible makes no mention of exalting ourselves and becoming Gods, but rather being subject to God and enjoying Him in all His glory.

I would personally say that it is not glorifying to God to do good works and follow his Word, only in an attempt to ultimately glorify your own being. If through the glorification of God you are actually seeking to better your own standing and gain power, then you actually practicing idolatry by placing yourself in equal standing with God through your actions. You idolize yourself, and believe you can be equal with God.

This Mormon doctrine contradicts the teachings laid out in the Bible. In Isaiah 43:10-11 it states, "Before me no God was formed, nor will there be one after me. I, even I am the Lord, and apart from me there is no Savior". So if God is God, and he is the only God, and there was no God before Him and there will be no God after Him, then how can Mormon doctrine teach that faithful Mormons will be "gods because they have all power" and "made ruler over many things"?

Why would God state an inerrant truth that He is and will be the only God, and then contradict that statement later? I would argue that this is a direct contradiction to the Bible, and therefore again cannot be true.

Smart on Earth = Smart in Heaven

There is also a requirement of intelligence and study that plays into attaining the celestial kingdom. Mormons believe "Whatever principles of intelligence we attain unto in this life, it will rise with us in the resurrection. And if a person gains more knowledge and intelligence in this life through his diligence and obedience than another, he will have so much the advantage in the world to come" Doctrine & Covenants 130:18-19.

For this reason, all through high school Mormons are required to attend Seminary classes. For several years I went to seminary classes every weekday morning, starting at 6am. Frankly, it was far too early in the morning for me to recall much of what I learned there. To relate back to the earlier discussions on grace – if Mormons must do good works to gain entry into the celestial kingdom, wouldn't it naturally follow that they also need to be diligent in their studies of the Mormon doctrine to attain this kingdom as well? The answer is yes, as you can only take the intelligence into heaven that you possess on earth.

But the Celestial Kingdom does not end there. The Doctrine & Covenants proceeds to describe the nature of the Celestial Kingdom in Doctrine & Covenants 130:6-7, "The angels do not reside on a planet like this earth; But they reside in the presence of God, on a globe like a sea of glass and fire, where all things for their glory are manifest, past, present, and future, and are continually before the Lord." As said before, it is believed that entry into the Celestial kingdom allows the person of entry the ability to constantly reside with God.

If you recall, the Book of Mormon was translated through the use of the Urim and Thummim stones. These stones are generally thought of within religious circles as an oracle, divine in nature. These stones manifest themselves again in Doctrine & Covenants 130:8-9 and become another very important part of Mormon beliefs.

"The place where God resides is a great Urim and Thummim. This earth, in its sanctified and immortal state, will be made like unto crystal and will be a Urim and Thummim to the inhabitants who dwell thereon, whereby all things pertaining to an inferior kingdom, or all kingdoms of a lower order, will manifest to those who dwell on it; and this earth will be Christ's."

These verses provide a bit more insight regarding nature of the three kingdoms. All inferior kingdoms will be transparent to the higher kingdoms in the order, as those in the Celestial Kingdom will be able to view the happenings of kingdoms beneath them.

Middle Heaven

The Terrestrial kingdom is considered to be middle heaven (I'm beginning to feel like I'm in Lord of the Rings). This kingdom is reserved for those people who believe in Jesus, but were not sufficiently good or worthy in their life.

Furthermore, those people who reject the teachings of the Mormon Church in their physical life, but accept the teachings in the spirit world will inherit the Terrestrial kingdom. (This thought is incorporated into the Mormon belief in baptisms for the dead, which will be discussed later in this book).

There are some conditions to this kingdom. The Mormon Church believes that within the Terrestrial kingdom, people will enjoy the presence of the Son but will not feel the fullness of the father – again as two separate beings – and these people will minister to those in the Telestial kingdom.

The Lowest Heaven

The Telestial kingdom is the lowest level of Heaven, reserved for those who profess that they follow Jesus but willfully reject His teachings. The people in this kingdom will be those people who were murderers, liars, sorcerers, adulterers, and generally the wicked people on Earth in their mortal life.

These people have come clean again through their suffering, and are therefore allowed to enjoy the glories of Telestial Heaven, rather than being sent to hell. Many Mormons will contend that they believe in grace because these people will go to heaven merely for the sake of their faith. However, I would say again that the Bible does not mention levels of heaven and specifically speaks against works, so the Mormon concept of grace must be decisively different from mainstream Christianity.

There are again conditions and limitations of this lowest level of Heaven. These inhabitants will be cast into Hell until the end of the Millennium (the 1000 years spoken of in the Doctrine & Covenants), and will only be resurrected to Telestial bodies after the Second Resurrection. These people will be servants of God, but God and Jesus will not dwell with them.

There is actually one level below the three levels of Heaven. This is a place that most would consider to be Hell. Satan and the Angels who followed them are referred to as the Sons of Perdition. Those people who said they believed in God (in their pre-mortal life, as believed by Mormons) to gain a mortal body, but rejected God in their mortal life will be Sons of Perdition.

"There are they who are sons of perdition, of whom I say that it had been better for them to never have been born; for they are vessels of wrath, doomed to suffer the wrath of God, with the devil and his angels in eternity; Concerning whom I have said there is no forgiveness in this world nor in the world to come – having denied the Holy Spirit after having received it, and having denied the Only Begotten Son of the Father, having crucified him unto themselves and put him to an open shame" Doctrine & Covenants 76:32-35.

Answering the Tough Questions

One reason why the Mormon Church appeals to many people is because they provide answers. They provide answers to controversial topics, making people feel better about what may happen after they or loved ones die.

For example, in my study of scripture, there is no place where God describes what happens to children who die. This question is simply unanswered. Are we supposed to know the answer? Did God not give us an answer in the Bible for a reason? If the Bible is the inerrant Word of God, then I would say yes. God told us exactly what we needed to know – nothing more and nothing less.

But this is difficult for so many people to grasp. It is within our nature to constantly be seeking answers to the questions that burn our souls, but we must be very careful with how and where we choose to get the answers we seek. Mormonism fills in these gaps through their revelations, providing the answers that people sometimes feel they need to hear, in the absence of answers within mainstream Christianity.

Some such answers are given with regards to death and non-believers or children in Doctrine & Covenants 137:7-10, saying "Thus came the voice of the Lord unto me, saying: all who would have died without a knowledge of this gospel, who would have received it if they had been permitted to tarry, shall be heirs to the celestial kingdom of God; Also all that shall die henceforth without a knowledge of it, who would have received it with all their hearts, shall be heirs of that kingdom; For I, the Lord, *will judge all men according to their works*, according to the desire of their hearts. And I also beheld that all children who die before they arrive at the years of accountability are saved in the celestial kingdom of heaven."

While this gives people that warm and fuzzy feeling, is it real? Is that what God said? Mainstream Christianity will agree that the Bible is the sole, divine word of God. God meant to say the things written therein, so He did. It is not in the nature of man to forego intelligence and not seek answers to our burning questions.

We always want to explore deeper and know more. As Christians, however, I would argue that we have to understand that there are principles in this world that we cannot understand, and things beyond our comprehension. In the absence of Biblical explanation, you cannot simply make up answers to those questions which you do not understand.

There are some things which are not meant to be answered or understood entirely, and we have to agree that there are some secrets which will simply reside in heaven. If you have ever stared at the stars at night looking into the sky, you will know this feeling. There is infinite darkness, eternal black, millions of glowing orbs. To me, God is like the sky – something that I know to exist, but I can never entirely understand the vastness that encompasses Him.

Mormons are not satisfied with what God has provided through the Bible, and through revelations they add to his Word. Whether or not you accept the Mormon doctrine as the truth is a personal choice, but I place the Bible at the forefront of Christianity and look to that Word for answers.

Again I will turn to Deuteronomy 4:2, saying, "Ye shall not add unto the word which I command you, neither shall ye diminish ought from it, that ye may keep the commandments of the Lord your God which I command you." If God says we cannot add to His Word, then we cannot add to it. Simple as that.

Zion

So what exactly is Zion? Throughout the Mormon scriptures, there is reference to a place called Zion, and an organization also referred to as the United Order. In the Doctrine & Covenants there are many references to Zion, particularly as Joseph Smith is establishing the church. However, Zion really has several meanings within the Mormon faith, several of which we will explain here.

The Great Utopia on Earth

In the LDS Church, Zion is Utopia, often referred to as 'New Jerusalem'. It is a society of righteous people, where the United Order is the agency amongst the people responsible for ensuring that every member has a good quality of life, and the separation of social classes is nonexistent. In essence, it is a socialistic society where every person is responsible for the welfare of everyone else, and there are no 'haves' and 'have not's'.

In the Book of Mormon and the Pearl of Great Price, Enoch founded a city for the righteous descendants of Adam, "And Enoch continued his preaching in righteousness unto the people of God. And it came to pass in his days, that he built a city that was called the City of Holiness, even Zion" Book of Mormon, Moses 7:19.

The people of this city were so good, righteous and pure of heart that the entire city was taken from the earth and put up in heaven, "And it came to pass that the Lord showed unto Enoch all the inhabitants of the earth; and he beheld, and lo, Zion, in process of time, was taken up into heaven." Book of Mormon, Moses 7:21.

In the Second Coming, Mormons believe that Zion will be restored to the Earth. They believe that Zion is to be located in Missouri, as stated in Doctrine & Covenants 57:1-2, "Hearken, O ye elders of my church, saith the Lord your God, who have assembled yourselves together, according to my commandments, in this land, which is the land of Missouri, which is the land I have appointed and consecrated for the gathering of the saints. Wherefore, this is the land of promise, and the place for the city of Zion."

They also believe that this is the place where Adam and Eve lived after being cast out of the Garden of Eden, and is referred to in the Mormon scripture as Adam-ondi-Ahman. "Spring Hill is named by the Lord Adam-ondi-Ahman, because, said he, it is the place where Adam shall come to visit his people, or the Ancient of Days shall sit, as spoken of by Daniel the prophet" Doctrine & Covenants 116:1.

Headline: Zion to be in Missouri

In Doctrine & Covenants 63:24-37, it was revealed to Joseph Smith that the people of the church were supposed to purchase the land to create Zion. "Wherefore, I the Lord will that you should purchase the lands, that you may have advantage of the world, that you may have claim on the world, that they may not be stirred up unto anger…wherefore, the land of Zion shall not be obtained but by purchase or by blood, otherwise there is none inheritance for you. And if by purchase, behold you are blessed. And if by blood, as you are forbidden to shed blood, lo, your enemies are upon you and ye shall be scourged from city to city…" In this portion of the Mormon scripture, God is actually commanding the Mormon people to purchase land to form the new Zion.

Headline: Just Kidding, Zion just means Pure of Heart

In the early church formation, however, Mormons were cast out of Missouri and Zion was never literally formed there as they had originally intended and prophesized. Later in Doctrine & Covenants 97:21 it was said, "Therefore, verily, thus saith the Lord, let Zion rejoice, for this is Zion – the pure in heart." As shown here, Zion later came to mean just the pure in heart, and the specific location for Zion in Missouri was somewhat dismissed.

However, regardless of the nature of the great Zion that Mormons believe will exist one day, they still believe in judging each other and their actions based upon gaining entry into this place. Doctrine & Covenants 64:38-40, "For it shall come to pass that the inhabitants of Zion shall judge all things pertaining to Zion. And liars and hypocrites shall be proved by them, and they who are not apostles and prophets shall be know. And even the bishop, who is a judge, and his counselors, if they are not faithful in their stewardships shall be condemned, and others shall be planted in their stead. For behold, I say unto you that Zion shall flourish, and the glory of the Lord shall be upon her." Even in Zion, the actions of the Mormon people are paramount to their existence there. They will be condemned for their actions and removed from office if they do not live up to the standards of Zion.

These standards or laws of Zion further emulate the principle of works, as presented in the LDS church. "And Zion cannot be built up unless it is by the principles of the law of the celestial kingdom; otherwise I cannot receive her unto myself" Doctrine & Covenants 105:5. Zion cannot exist unless by the principles of the Mormon Church, specifically those pertaining to the celestial kingdom as outlined in the Salvation portion of this book.

THE NOT-SO-MORMON WORD

Up to this point, I have not made reference to the Journal of Discourses. There are twenty six volumes in the Journal of Discourses written by multiple early church leaders and dating up to 1886, decades after the original establishment of the Mormon Church.

It was a semimonthly publication that Mormon churchgoers could subscribe to, like a religious newspaper or magazine.

Spreading the Word

Originally the Journal of Discourses was printed for distribution in England, to inform English members of the Mormon Church of those events happening in Salt Lake City, Utah. Since there was no internet or conferencing capabilities as we have today, much of the information provided to the LDS churches of England came through these journals.

Brigham Young himself actually authorized the printing of these Journals. Eventually there were 1,438 speeches recorded in these journals, 390 of which came from Brigham Young.

No Longer Official

The Church of Jesus Christ of Latter Day Saints now offers the following view on the Journal of Discourses, "The Journal of Discourses is not an official publication of The Church of Jesus Christ of Latter-day Saints. It is a compilation of sermons and other materials from the early years of the Church, which were transcribed and then published. It includes practical advice as well as doctrinal discussion, some of which is speculative in nature and some of which is only of historical interest. ... Questions have been raised about the accuracy of some transcriptions. Modern technology and processes were not available for verifying the accuracy of transcriptions, and some significant mistakes have been documented. The Journal of

Discourses includes interesting and insightful teachings by early Church leaders; however, by itself it is not an authoritative source of Church doctrine."

I have not made reference to the Journals of Discourse up to this point because while they were incredibly influential and are an indication of the original beliefs established by the Mormon faith, Mormons today maintain that these documents are not part of their cannon and not representative of what they believe. For that reason, this will be the only chapter in which I will mention the Journals and their contents.

Again, I admit that I was never taught from the Journal of Discourses in my youth. There are some churches which share and teach the contents of these journals and some which do not, and most of the contents found in these journals are very theological and not for the understanding of children.

We Don't Believe it, We Just Cite it.

First, any Christian on the planet can argue that any speech transcribed or documented may at some point be subject to an error in printing, transcription, etc. Based on the Church's official statement about the Journal of Discourses, one would be led to believe that the Mormon Church has discredited this journal and thrown it out of their teachings entirely.

False. This becomes incredibly confusing because while Mormons will not site it as cannon in their official scriptures, they continue to reference excerpts from these speeches within their teaching. Want proof? Go to www.lds.org and in the 'Search' bar, type in 'Journal of Discourses'. The last time I did this search, six hundred and thirty-three references to the Journal of Discourses were referenced and included in speeches and writings by the church in the modern day.

While many Mormons will stand there and say that these early recordings of teachers in the church's history were subject to error, opinion and interpretation, and are not considered doctrine, they are still referenced and utilized within their own LDS-approved website as a source of viable and teachable information. That seems a bit hypocritical to me.

We were wrong. Twenty-six times.

Furthermore, if the teachings of the Journal of Discourses were so unpopular and unfounded, why would the LDS church have published twenty six different volumes of this literature? It seems that at twenty six different times, the magnitude of the speeches given by the church leaders were significant enough to warrant not only documenting and transcribing these speeches, but also publishing them.

Had the church leaders who gave these speeches been unhappy with the record of their teachings, wouldn't they also have gone to the transcribers and recorders in an effort to fix what had been written? I know that if someone misquoted me, I would want them to correct the error. Yet, these not only were published and widely accepted, but continued to be published twenty six times without recourse.

Written by the Big Guys

Further yet, the Book of Mormon and Doctrine & Covenants readily accept within their own text that they were written by man and subject to human error. Yet, those books are still in the Mormon cannon of scripture. Why are those particular books, also subject to human error by their own accord, considered to be acceptable, while the teachings of those scriptures by high-level church officials were not?

These Journals of Discourse were not simply written by some random church leaders, either. In fact, the very first volume of the Journal of Discourses was started by none other than the great Brigham Young, a man so esteemed in the Mormon Church that they named the single most popular LDS University after him. Hardly a person I would consider to be unimportant or insignificant.

Okay, so let's say that these speeches were the open interpretation of the leaders of the LDS church and as such must be thrown out completely. Similarly, could we not say that every single Sunday the Bishop, or your

Pastor for that matter, provides you with a kernel of insight into your faith based upon his interpretation of the scriptures? Do we then just throw out everything that the Bishop or Pastor says? Of course not.

We make the assumption that everything they are teaching us is based on a fundamental truth. It is my opinion that while the teachings in the Journal of Discourses may be divisive, they still possess a backbone of truth and insight into historical Mormon teachings. They also demonstrate the Mormon Church's ability to alter their teachings to appeal to a broader spectrum of people.

I have read the Journal of Discourses. The Journals which I read were from the online library of Brigham Young University, containing the actual scanned copies of every page of every Journal of Discourse written.

I make this note because I want to be clear that I did not receive the information about these Journals from an anti-Mormon source, but rather from the library of the largest source for pro-Mormon literature and teachings in the world. For those who would dispute these teachings, I would encourage you to review these documents yourself. What was written in these infamous Journals of Discourses?

There is a very specific reason why I have waited until this point to include the teachings of the Journal of Discourse. To me, these sermons and speeches are the most explosive of the documentation I have had the opportunity to sift through. They speak loudly to the prominent teachings of the early Mormon Church, and are irrefutably powerful.

They also explain the beliefs of break-off factions of Mormonism, such as the FLDS (Fundamental Latter Day Saints) Church, which has been popular in the news due to their continued practices of polygamy.

Now that you have had an introduction to the Mormon views on original sin, grace, the nature of God, salvation, and other such topics, these Journals of Discourse piece all of this information in a way that few other documents in the LDS archives can.

The Origins of God: God is an Exalted Man

In the Journal of Discourses, Volume 6, Pages 3-10, Joseph Smith speaks to the origins of God. Note, I have not said the nature of God, but actually the very of origins of God, answering the question "Where did God come from?"

Mormons believe that God is just as man is now. God, just as Jesus did (remember they are considered two separate beings) walked an earth as a man, performed good works and received his exaltation. He was then promoted to God, where he sits on the throne and presides over the lives of each of us.

"God was once, as we are now, an exhalted man, and sits enthroned in yonder heavens. That is the great secret. If the vail was rent today, and the great God who holds this world in orbit and who upholds all worlds and all things by his power, was to make himself visible, - I say, if you were to see him today, you would see him like a man in form – like yourselves, in all the person, image and very form as man; for Adam was created in the very fashion, image and likeness of God, and received instruction from, and walked, talked and conversed with him, as one man talks and communes with another...God himself, the father of us all, dwelt on an earth, the same as Jesus Christ himself did..." JOD, Volume 6, Page 3-4, Joseph F. Smith. This view of God as simply an exalted man goes hand in hand with the Mormon viewpoint of the celestial kingdom of heaven, and the promises of possessing the powers of God.

You are Equal to Jesus

This message speaks of God much, much differently than mainstream Christians do. In fact, Mormons do not believe in God the same way we do at all. Being a God is something completely attainable.

"You have got to learn how to be Gods yourselves, and to be kings and priests to God, the same as all Gods have done before you, namely, by going from one small degree to another, and from a small capacity to a great one, from grace to grace, from exaltation to exaltation, until you attain to the resurrection of the dead, and are able to dwell in everlasting burnings and sit in glory, as do those who sit enthroned in everlasting power." JOD, Volume 6, Page 3-4, Joseph F. Smith.

In essence, God was a spirit child of another world who gained exaltation, and then begot us as spirit children and became God over us. Likewise, we too can have spirit children and become God over them. In this way, they have created a huge circle, where people can become Gods who create more people who also can become Gods, and create even more people who become Gods. "There never was a time when there were not spirits; for they are co-equal with our Father in Heaven." JOD, Volume 6, pages 6, Joseph F. Smith.

In this way, we actually become equal to Jesus. Jesus is simply one of our spirit brothers, begotten of the same God as we were. Mirroring this teaching by Joseph Smith, Brigham Young also spoke to the origins of Jesus.

"When the Virgin Mary conceived the child Jesus, the Father had begotten him in his own likeness. He was not begotten by the Holy Ghost. And who is the Father? He is the first of the human family; and when he took a tabernacle, it was begotten by *his Father* in heaven, after the same manner as the tabernacles of Cain, Abel and the rest of the sons and daughters of Adam and Eve." JOD, Volume 1, Page 50, Brigham Young.

This statement first speaks against the concept of a miraculous conception as believed in most Christian faiths. This is also in line with their current belief that God, Jesus and the Holy Spirit are three separate beings, and Jesus is the literal Son of God.

Since we are all spirit children of God and Jesus is no higher than ourselves, we can inherit all of the glories that most Christian faiths reserve for Jesus alone. "They shall be heirs of God and joint-heirs with Jesus Christ. What is it? To inherit the same power, the same glory, and the same exaltation, until you arrive at the station of a God and ascend the throne of eternal power, the same as those who have gone before." JOD, Volume 6, Page 4, Joseph Smith.

Becoming the God of Gods

However, the staircase of exaltation does not end there. From that point, it is possible to be exalted even further. This means that God is not necessarily at the highest level he can be, being that God was once subject to a God.

You can become exalted above your current level of exaltation, as your spirit children are exalted and thus exalt you to an even higher level. It's like the pyramid scheme of heaven.

"What did Jesus do? Why, I do the things I saw my Father do when worlds came rolling into existence. My Father worked out his kingdom with fear and trembling, and I must do the same; and when I get my kingdom, I shall present it to my Father, so that he may obtain kingdom upon kingdom, and it will exalt him in glory. He will then take a higher exaltation, and I will take his place, and thereby become exalted myself. So that Jesus treads in the track of his Father, and inherits what God did before; and God is thus glorified and exalted in the salvation and exaltation of all his children. When you climb a ladder, you must begin at the bottom and ascent step by step until you arrive at the top; and so it is with the principles of the Gospel: your must begin with the first, and go on until you learn all the principles of exaltation." JOD, Volume 6, Page 4, Joseph F. Smith.

Plurality of God

In this context, you cannot deny that Mormons believe on some level in the plurality of Gods. Not only are God, Jesus and the Holy Spirit considered to be separate, but they are not the only ones. If God came from a God just as we come from a God, and we can become Gods to spawn more Gods, then you cannot deny a belief in multiple Gods.

Mormons cannot deny the act of exaltation and becoming a God, and therefore I would say that they do not deny these principles taught in the early Mormon Church and must inherently believe in a plurality of Gods.

The Grand Council

Within the sixth volume of the Journal of Discourse, Joseph Smith also spoke about a different type of beginning of the world than that displayed in the book of Genesis in the Bible. "The head God called together the Gods and sat in a grand council to bring forth the world" JOD, Volume 6, Page 5, Joseph F. Smith.

I would again say that this is again in line with the Mormon teachings. After all, Mormons do believe in a preexisting life, they deny original sin and they maintain that our present lives are a test. That is their principle for salvation and subsequent exaltation.

Different Worlds

But how do those in the spirit world vary from those who have had tabernacles, or physical bodies? There are two worlds, one that exists for those who have received bodies, and one for those who remain in the spirit world and do not have bodies.

"Thrones, kingdoms, crowns, principalities and powers in the celestial and eternal worlds, and the fullness of the presence of the Father, and of His Son Jesus Christ, are reserved for resurrected beings, who dwell in immortal flesh. The world of resurrected beings and the world of spirits are two distinct spheres, as much so as our own sphere is distinct from that of the spirit world. Where then does the spirit go, on its departure from its earthly tabernacle? It passes to the next sphere of human existence, called the world of spirits, a vail being drawn between us in the flesh, and that world of spirits. Well, says one, is there no more than one place in the spirit world? Yes, there are many places and degrees in that world, as in this." JOD, Volume 1, Page 9, Pratt.

These separate worlds are reflected in the current Mormon belief that Jesus and his angels descended into hell to preach the gospel to those who were damned. "Jesus Christ, when absent from his flesh, did not ascend to the Father to be crowned, and enthroned in power. Why? Because he had not yet a resurrected body, and had therefore a mission to perform in another sphere. Where then did he go? To the world of spirits, to wicked, sinful spirits, who died in their sins, being swept off by the flood of Noah. The thief on the cross, who died at the same time, also went to the same world, and to the same particular place in the same world, for he was a sinner, and would of course go to the prison of the condemned, there to await the ministry of that Gospel which had failed to reach his case while on earth." JOD, Volume 1, Page 9, Pratt.

"To say that Jesus Christ dwells in the world of spirits, with those whose bodies are dead, would not be the truth. He is not there. He only staid there till the third day" JOD, Volume 1, Page 10, Pratt. This leads to the Mormon belief that people can accept the gospel in the spirit world, and is the ultimate reason for their controversial practice in baptism for the dead.

Along the lines of those who have passed, there have always been questions about what happens to children when they die. As we have said, Mormons offer comfort to those grieving for that loss by confirming that children who die before their age of accountability will see the glories of heaven.

This was preached by Joseph Smith, "A question may be asked – "Will mothers have their children in eternity?" Yes! Yes! Mothers, you shall have your children; for they shall have eternal life; for their debt is paid. There is no damnation awaits them, for they are in the spirit. But as the child dies, so shall it rise from the dead, and be forever living in the learning of God. It will never grow, it will still be the child, in the same precise form as it appeared before it died out of its mother's arms, but possessing all the intelligence of a God." JOD, Volume 6, Page 10, Joseph F. Smith.

The Adam-God Theory

There is one particular theory created in these Journals of Discourse which is highly controversial, both in the LDS church and in Christianity. This old teaching of the early Mormon Church, said to have originated from Brigham Young, is called the Adam-God theory. This theory states that Adam, the father of all man, is actually God.

As preached by Brigham Young, "The infidel world have concluded that if what the Apostles wrote about his father and mother be true, and the present marriage discipline acknowledged by Christendom be correct, then Christians must believe that God is the father of an illegitimate son, in the person of Jesus Christ! ... Our Father in Heaven begat all the spirits that ever were, or ever will be, upon this earth; and they were born spirits in the eternal world. Then the Lord by His power and wisdom organized the mortal tabernacle of man. We were made first spiritual, and afterwards temporal...When our father Adam came into the Garden of Eden, he came into it with a celestial body, and brought Eve, *one of his wives*, with him. He helped to make and organize this world. He is Michael, the Archangel, the ancient of days! He is our Father and our God, and the only God with whom we have to do." JOD, Volume 1, Page 50, Brigham Young.

It should be noted that this particular view from the LDS church was later publically denounced. As Spencer W. Kimball wrote in the November 1976 article of *Ensign Magazine*, "We hope that you who teach in the various organizations, whether on the campuses or in our chapels, will always teach the orthodox truth. We warn you against the dissemination of doctrines which are not according to the scriptures and which are alleged to have been taught by some of the General Authorities of past generations. Such, for instance, is the Adam-God theory. We denounce that theory and hope that everyone will be cautioned against this and other kinds of false doctrine."

This is not a current belief of the Mormon Church, but it is representative of the Church's history as a one-time undeniable truth, and another example of denouncing an unpopular belief.

God was a Polygamist

This last passage from the Journals of Discourse brings up another viable point. Eve is considered to be *one* of the wives of Adam in the early teaching of the church. Orson Pratt spoke of the practice of polygamy in an extensive speech recorded in the Journal of Discourses.

As you will see throughout this speech, plurality of wives was very fundamental to the Mormon belief. After all, if God begat hundreds of spirit children (us), he must have had many spirit wives to create those children.

The very nature of God addressed in the Journal of Discourse was polygamous, and polygamy was nearly a requirement of salvation. "...the Latter Day Saints have embraced the doctrine of a plurality of wives, as a part of their religious faith...we will show you that it is incorporated as a part of our religion, and necessary for our exaltation to the fullness of the Lord's glory in the eternal world." JOD, Volume 1, Page 54, Orson Pratt.

The goal of polygamy as practiced by God was to increasingly multiply his spirit children, just as Mormon men were encouraged to multiply their children and followers of the Mormon faith. "If one God can propagate his species, and raise up spirits after his own image and likeness, and call them his sons and daughters, so can all other Gods that become like him, do the same thing; consequently there will be many Fathers, and there will be many families, and many sons and daughters; and they will be the children of those glorified, celestial beings that are counted worthy to be Gods." JOC, Volume 1, Page 57, Orson Pratt.

Mormons believe in celestial marriage, or sealing to one another for eternity. This is their covenant of marriage. It was the Mormon Church's goal through the promotion of polygamy to create children who would be sealed to you on earth and in heaven, and that those children may have the hopes of becoming exalted and later Gods. The more children you could have that became exalted, the higher and higher you yourself could be exalted.

"By virtue of the everlasting and eternal covenant of marriage, they will continue to increase and multiply to all ages of eternity, to raise up beings after their own order, and in their own likeness and image, germs of intelligence, that are destines, in their times and seasons, to become not only sons of God, but Gods themselves." JOD, Volumes 1, Page 59, Orson Pratt.

Again, Mormons claim this to be the promise of Abraham. In fact, Orson Pratt even spoke against mainstream Christianity, considering those who did not agree with the practice of polygamy to be ignorant. "Here then, was a foundation laid for the fulfillment of the great and grand promise concerning the multiplicity of his seed. It would have been rather a slow process, if Abraham had been confined to one wife, like some of those narrow, contracted nations of modern Christianity…and even those who have only one wife, cannot get rid of their covetousness, and get their little hearts large enough to share their property with a numerous family; they are so penurious, and so narrow and contracted in their feelings, that they take every possible care not to have their families large." JOD Volume 1, Page 60, Orson Pratt. It is Pratt's belief here that men who have only one wife cannot help but have a covetous and selfish heart, not wanting to provide more for more people.

Blood Atonement

Another interesting point established by Brigham Young in the early days of the church was called Blood Atonement. Throughout the establishment of the Mormon faith and still today, there has been a history of violence against the Mormon people. This is primarily because of their relationship with mainstream Christianity and their variations of and additions to the Bible, which Christians hold so sacred in their hearts.

I find it interesting that at the time of such great persecution, Joseph Smith recorded revelations from God regarding how to handle those who persecute them. "And in whatsoever place ye shall enter, and they receive you not in my name, ye shall leave a cursing instead of a blessing, by casting off the dust of your feet against them as a testimony, and cleansing your feet by the wayside. And it shall come to pass that whosoever shall lay their hands upon you in violence, ye shall command to be smitten in my name; and, behold, I will smite them according to your words, in mine own due time. And whosoever shall go to law with thee shall be cursed by the law" Doctrine & Covenants 24:15-17.

While it is my personal belief that God is a powerful and mighty God, I also believe that God is a good and loving God. It is not in line with the teachings of the New Testament to curse your neighbor.

The Old Testament offered a much stronger and harsher recourse against those who would speak ill of Christianity, but in the New Testament, Jesus creates a much different picture of kindness towards man. "Bless him which persecute you: bless, and curse not" Romans 12:14.

The Bible speaks directly against doing that which the Doctrine & Covenants commands. It does not seem in the character of God to permit men to go around cursing those people who do not believe the Mormon faith, in the name of God – especially when he has instructed otherwise.

In Mormon Doctrine, God provides instructions regarding those things which are to be done to non-believers. "And in whatsoever house ye enter, and they receive you, leave your blessing upon that house. And in whatsoever house ye enter, and they receive you not, ye shall depart speedily from that house, and shake off the dust of your feet as testimony against them. And you shall be filled with joy and gladness; and know this, that in the day of judgment you shall be judges of that house, and condemn them; And it shall be more tolerable for the heathen in the day of judgment, than for that house; therefore, gird up your loins and be faithful, and ye shall overcome all things, and be lifted up at the last day. Even so. Amen" Doctrine & Covenants 75:19-22.

This text paints a very different picture of God and the Mormon people. People of the Mormon faith, as dictated in the Doctrine & Covenants, actually believe that in the final days, they will be the judges of those people who stand against their beliefs. This seems to go against the strong Mormon (and Biblical, for that matter) principles of forgiveness.

How can you forgive people for their errors and sins in life, but then stand and condemn them upon judgment day? In Matthew 7:1-2, it says "Judge not, that ye be not judged. For with what judgment ye judge, ye shall be judged: and with what measure ye mete, it shall be measured to you again." If the Bible commands that we do not judge, then what authority is provided in the Doctrine & Covenants that Mormons alone can stand in judgment?

Perhaps most commonly known by mainstream Christians are the popular Mormon laws of morality. Of course, in no way am I condemning the

Mormon belief in living a moral life. I have many friends and family members in the Mormon faith who I would say are some of the kindest and most moral people I have ever met in my life, and I could only hope to be equal to them in their quest of a moral lifestyle (as a result of my relationship with God, and not to try and gain a spot in celestial heaven, of course). More than any other, I would suggest that these laws differentiate them as a faith and as a people.

These laws of morality are outlined in Doctrine & Covenants 136:19-24, "And if any man shall seek to build up himself, and seeketh not my counsel, he shall have not power and his folly shall be made manifest. Seek ye; and keep all your pledges with one another; and covet not that which is thy brother's. Keep yourselves from evil to take the name of the Lord in vain...Cease to contend one with another; cease to speak evil one of another. Cease drunkenness; and let your words tend to edifying one another." These are mostly basic principles, understood and accepted by most of Christianity. The one principle that Mormons may be most famous for is not drinking at all, even for sacraments. This is commanded of them in the Doctrine & Covenants, and not abiding by these principles could cost Mormons their salvation.

These laws of morality become more specific, saying, "If thou borrowest of thy neighbor, thou shalt restore that which thou has borrowed; and if thou canst not repay then go straightway and tell thy neighbor, lest he condemn thee. If thou shalt find that which thy neighbor has lost, thou shalt make diligent search until thou shalt deliver it to him again" Doctrine & Covenants 136:25-26. These two laws of neighborly goodness again lend themselves toward the utopian society of Zion, a community of people dependent upon each other for spiritual growth. The cornerstone of this dependency and great utopian society is the principle of moralism, which spreads into many areas of Mormon belief

The reason for bringing up the Mormon principle of moralism is because it directly relates with the early principle of Blood Atonement. Mormons consider murder to be an unforgiveable sin – if one commits murder, there is no grace. The Blood Atonement is an answer to this sin, allowing for a sacrifice to be made to pay the debt.

Blood Atonement is spoken of by Brigham Young and recorded in the Journals of Discourses. By sacrificing your own blood and life, you can atone for the sin of murder and be forgiven. "…If they had their eyes open to see their true condition, they would be perfectly willing to have their blood spilt upon the ground, that the smoke thereof might ascent to heaven as an offering for their sins; and the smoking incense would atone for their sins, whereas, if such is not the case, they will stick to them and remain upon them in the spirit world…I know that there are transgressors who, if they knew themselves, and the only condition upon which they can obtain forgiveness, would beg of their brethren to shed their blood, that the smoke thereof might ascend to God as an offering to appease the wrath that is kindled against them, and that the law might have its course. I will say I have had men come to me and offer their lives to atone for their sins" JOD, Volume 3, Page 53, Brigham Young.

This act of sacrifice is compared to similar acts in the Old Testament when alter sacrifices were made to God. Christians would argue that through the ultimate sacrifice of Jesus Christ in the New Testament, we were given grace so that our sins are covered in the blood of Christ and as such, no further sacrifices are required. This speaks to a lack of grace even in the early foundations of the LDS church. The one final payment option to counter your transgressions is basically suicide, which counters all Christian teachings related to taking one's own life.

It should be noted that the Mormon Church denounces this belief, and does not practice this today. However, it is interesting that Idaho and Utah (both states with a strong Mormon population) the firing squad has been an option in capital punishment. It was not until March of 2004 in Utah and July of 2009 in Idaho that laws were passed to ban execution by firing squad.

For two states who hail many Mormon followers claiming not to believe in the Journals of Discourse or the Blood Atonement therein, it seems to have taken quite some time to remove this law which would support that belief. These are a few of many of the touchy subjects brought to light by the Journals of Discourse. Again, most Mormons will maintain that these speeches were transcribed incorrectly and are subject to error.

However, if they are referenced in any capacity within speeches or literature provided by the Mormon Church, then they must hold some level of truth to Mormon believers. These texts, while volatile in nature, speak a great deal to the temperament upon the establishment of the church. They also speak a great deal to the theology of the early church, and have many roots in the doctrine taught today.

In my opinion, the early church seemed to be much louder regarding their non-streamlined Christian beliefs. There has been a big push in the LDS church to appear more 'Christian' in recent years, and missionaries even knock on doors, introducing themselves and saying that 'their beliefs do not differ far from all Christians'. The Mormon Church of today keeps very quiet about their beliefs on many of the more controversial subjects, making them even more difficult to ascertain. Do not be fooled.

The Christianity Debate

As can be anticipated, there is much debate surrounding the 'Christian' nature of the Mormon Church. If you were to ask me growing up whether or not I was Christian, I would have undoubtedly told you 'yes'. On that same note, my entire family – both sides – is also devoutly Mormon, and I would have told you that they are Christian as well.

In my experience, the 'Christian debate' largely stems from what you believe the definition of Christianity to be, and the nature of God. The name of the Mormon Church is actually The Church of Jesus Christ of Latter-day Saints. The Merriam-Webster dictionary defines a Christian as 'one who professes belief in the teachings of Jesus Christ'. This definition is very broad, and does not place any restrictions or terms on Christianity.

LDS members are taught to follow the teachings of Jesus, worshiping Christ, baptizing in Christ's name, and partaking of Sacrament to remember the body and blood of Christ. In fact, the third Article of Faith in the Mormon Church states "We believe that through the Atonement of Christ, all mankind may be saved . . ."

The famous Mormon Tabernacle Choir sings Christian hymns to exalt Christ. All Mormons have a commitment to morality, goodness and strong families. It would seem to be a natural progression that these strong Christian principles would naturally indicate that Mormons engage in a Christian life.

Who is the 'Christ' in your 'Christian'?

There is disagreement amongst most Christians regarding the nature of the 'Mormon Gods'. Since Mormons clearly state that they believe that God the Father, Jesus Christ and the Holy Spirit are three individual entities, they are clearly stating that there are three Gods – or admitting that Jesus is lesser in importance and power than God. Many people of the LDS faith would argue that there is only one God, and that is God the Father. In this way, they would argue that there are three personages but only one literal God and while Jesus is the same in purpose, he is lesser in power than God.

This was always a highly debated point for me and my husband, as I could not understand why he refused to attend a Mormon Church. While I had no intention of trying to convert him to Mormonism and I was no longer a Mormon myself, I did want him to attend a Mormon Church with me to understand my upbringing and where I came from. To me, the more he understood my old faith and my family's faith, the more he understood me and he could help me in my Christian journey.

It took me until I wrote this book to sincerely understand this debate and be able to see his perspective on the issue. I thought he was being obstinate and simply unwilling to see another perspective of Christianity. As it turns out, that was not the case at all. The Christianity debate ultimately came down to the nature of God, and how we view Him. I don't believe that the question is really: Are Mormons Christian?

The question really becomes: Who is the 'Christ' in your 'Christian'? What I mean by this is – if the Mormon view of God is solely God the Father and the mainstream view of God is a triune God, then we are not worshipping the same God. It was not until only a few years ago that I heard for the first time that Jesus was God, and this idea baffled me. While in nearly all Christian denominations the triune view of God is the same, my husband understood that the LDS view was not the same as his own and feared going to a church and partaking in worship of a false God.

God is God. Jesus is God. The Holy Spirit is God. They are all God, three in one and one in three. Mainstream Christians believe in the statements made in the Nicene Creed. We believe that Jesus and the Holy Spirit are of one substance with the Father. I personally believe that since Mormons do not believe God to be of the same nature that mainstream Christians do, they do not believe in the same God and therefore are not categorically Christian.

Is the Bible the errant Word of God?

The root of the Mormon Church is their belief that the Bible is not the only Word of God. As discussed earlier, the Mormons believe in four total scriptures – the Book of Mormon, the Bible, the Doctrine & Covenants and the Pearl of Great Price. They contend that the Bible is the incomplete and errant Word of God, and that they have a more complete offering of God's teachings.

Again, most Christian churches will teach that the Bible is the inerrant and only Word of God. This further removes Mormonism from mainstream Christianity, and raises major questions within the Christian community regarding whether or not Mormons are again, actually categorically Christian.

Is Mormonism a Cult?

Now for the really hard question that I despise. Is Mormonism a cult? Well, the Merriam-Webster dictionary defines a cult as a "religion regarded as unorthodox or spurious", or a "system of religious beliefs and ritual". I would say that it is most likely a combination of the two. You cannot simply look at a "system of religious beliefs and ritual" to define a cult, because then all religious could be easily be called cults.

We all have beliefs and we all have rituals (take communion, baptism or prayer for example). However, Biblically-based mainstream Christian religions will firmly claim that Mormon beliefs are 'unorthodox and spurious', or false.

Most Christian denominations, while we practice differently, are rooted in the same biblical truths outlined in the Nicene Creed. Those who oppose these views that are a common root of truth and unity in Christianity are seen as untrue for that very reason.

Cults are associated with not only unorthodox beliefs, but also a form of mind control. These types of mind control would include control over a group of people's actions, information access, finances and thoughts.

Typically in order to control these actions, punishments must be rendered if rules are broken. If those are the categories of control to be exercised, let's look at the LDS church a little closer.

Control over Actions? The Mormon Church is highly concerned with the morality of their people. They do not permit alcohol consumption, caffeine consumption, tobacco consumption, foul speech or unchaste behaviors. While these are all actions in excess that are frowned upon in mainstream Christianity, mainstream churches generally do not punish members for their actions. Rather, mainstream Christian Churches take steps to be proactive and assist people in overcoming their vices, but do not withhold salvation as a result of those actions.

However, these poor behaviors would prevent a Mormon member from accessing the temple, and therefore prevent them from being able to perform the ordinances necessary for their salvation. Breaking church rules = losing your salvation. Frankly, I prefer to leave that type of judgment rendering in God's hands.

Control over Information? Mormons are discouraged from viewing or reading materials that are not approved by the LDS church. Mormons are also discouraged from reading scriptures that are not approved, including the NIV, ESV and other newer translations of the Bible. While these newer translations are much easier to understand, the LDS church maintains a level of fear within the Mormon society that these translations are false, as they are highly frowned upon by church leaders.

Any literature providing an insight of Mormon beliefs that is not approved by the church – even this very book – would be considered anti-Mormon and therefore sinful. Mormon missionaries are not even allowed to speak with the media unless it is approved by the church. Again, why is there a need to control the information going into and coming out of Mormon homes? The less mainstream Christians understand about Mormons, the more difficult it is to help them. I never knew the truth because I was never allowed to seek after it.

Control over Finances? Mormons are required to provide a full 10% tithe to the church. Failure to pay their tithe will force the LDS leaders to revoke their entry into the Mormon temples, again preventing them from performing the ordinances necessary to attain salvation. Not paying the church = losing your salvation. You either pay the literal price from your bank account, or you will pay the ultimate price in your life to come.

Control over Thoughts? All Mormons do not address each other as 'Mr.' or 'Ms.' at all. Instead, all members refer to each other as 'Brother' and 'Sister', saying 'Hello, Sister Smith' or 'Hello, Brother Cole'. These addresses create an attitude of community and an inner circle of trust in the church. There is also a communal belief that the Prophet of the Mormon Church is always correct and no one is to question his actions.

Those who question their doctrines or leaders are said to be anti-Mormon, and trying to create anti-Mormon sentiments in their society. They must repent of this grave sin or face excommunication, and potentially lose their chance at attaining celestial exaltation.

There are clearly major repercussions for speaking against the LDS church within the Mormon faith. There is also a very clear exercise of control over actions, information, finances and thoughts in the church. In fact, as I stand back, now a non-member of the Mormon Church and think about my childhood in the church, it is absolutely frightening to think back on how much control this church had over me and still has over my family.

The church receives every extra dime my family possesses and has created this false socialistic society of 'brothers' and 'sisters' amongst my family and others. Is Mormonism a cult? As much as it pains me to say so, yes, I believe that it is. It can be said that since these teachings are expressly different than those shared by mainstream Christianity and their views on the Bible, the Mormon Church is ultimately viewed as a non-Christian Church with penchant for cult-like control over individuals.

Baptism, Sacraments & the Holy Spirit

I walked into church, dressed in my Sunday best. I was only eight years old, so going to the temple was still a good ten years into the future. It was the same church we had always gone to, for as long as I could remember. The church was set up like a big circle.

Around the outside perimeter were all of the classrooms and offices. In the center near the front was the main chapel area where we held sacrament – what most people would refer to as a mass or service.

At the back of the chapel area were those collapsible walls, the type that would fold up like an accordion. On the other side of the accordion-style walls was a basketball court with shiny wood floors and a stage, for youth games, shows and meetings. Whenever we had the really big services like Christmas and Easter, they would fold up the walls and put folding chairs onto the basketball court area for overflow. On the other side of the stage were the men's and women's restrooms, and the baptismal font.

It was the morning I was supposed to get baptized. I was eight years old, and I had reached the age of accountability. I heard the running water and walked past the font. It looked like a really big bathtub, with stairs on either side. On the right side of the font was the women's restroom. On the left side of the font was the men's.

My dad walked into the men's room, and my mom grabbed my hand and led me into the women's room. In that room my mother pulled out a white robe. Well, it looked more like a jumpsuit made out of a white towel-like material, really. I put on the robe and pulled back my hair into a ponytail.

When I was finished getting ready, my mom led me to the stairs. You could actually get to the stairs right from the bathroom – I remember thinking that I had never seen that door before and it would be a perfect place to hide next time I didn't want to go to Sunday school. I wondered if they locked that door.

I began walking down the stairs, only to see that my Dad was already in the baptismal font, dressed in the same robe as I was, waiting for me. I am the oldest of three kids, so I had never gotten to go to my sibling's baptisms before. I had no trial run, and no real idea of what I was doing. I started walked the steps down into the water. Thinking it would be cold, I cringed a little, only to be pleasantly surprised that it was warm. Then again, the font looked like a bathtub so I should have seen that coming.

I faced my dad, and he faced me. In our church, I knew it was 'baptism by immersion for the remission of sins', so I knew what was coming. Dad was going to dunk me, and I was pretty nervous about it. "Are you ready?" he asked. "Yeah" I responded hesitantly. He put his hand around my waist and put his right hand in the air, and then said, "Having been commissioned of Jesus Christ, I baptize you in the name of the Father, and of the Son, and of the Holy Ghost. Amen."

Stepping back slightly, he put his hand over my hand, reached up to my face and helped me plug my nose, and then pushed me back into the water. His hand still behind my back to hold me, under I went. He pulled me straight back up, and I wiped the water from my eyes and looked at my dad. He was looking up at the Bishop who was standing outside of the font. He looked at my dad and shook his head.

My dad looked at me and said, "We have to do it again." "Why?" I asked. "Your feet came up," he said. So again, he put his arm behind my back and raised his right hand in the air, and repeated the same phrase. Under I went again, but this time I made sure to bend my knees so my feet wouldn't come up. I didn't want to do this a third time. When I came up again the second time I wiped my face, but this time both my dad and I turned to look at the bishop. He nodded his head in approval, and my dad looked at me and said, "You can go change now."

My mom met me in the ladies bathroom again, with a fresh change of clothes and a blow dryer. I was glad, because it was freezing in that bathroom. I changed clothes and re-did my hair, but I knew we weren't done yet. I walked out of the ladies room, all dressed and dry. My dad grabbed my hand and had me sit on a folding chair in a room. There were three other men, older men, which were in the room with me shortly after. My dad was there of course, and then the Bishop, and then two other elders in the church. They told me they were going to give me the gift of the Holy Spirit. They all put their hands on my head, and then said a prayer, giving me the Holy Ghost and asking the Holy Ghost to help me choose between right and wrong.

Just like that, it was all done. I was baptized and I had received the Holy Ghost. And from that moment on, I had zero sins and I was accountable for everything I did. Before we got in the car to go home, my mom gave me my first set of Mormon scriptures. They were the nice ones, brick red leather cover and gold-edged paper with tabs and my name etched in gold on the bottom right-hand corner. All four books were in one book so it was much larger than the traditional Bible, so my mom had bought me a carrying case as well. So lovely, I couldn't wait to show my friends.

We went home and my parents made a special dinner with mashed potatoes – my favorite – and they told me how proud they were of me. That is my memory from my baptism and receipt of the Holy Spirit in my childhood. Baptism is considered by the Mormon Church to be crucial to forgiveness and salvation. The ninth article of faith in the Mormon Church says, "We believe that the first principles and ordinances of the Gospel are: first, Faith in the Lord Jesus Christ; second, Repentance; third, Baptism by immersion for the remission of sins; fourth, Laying on of hands for the gift of the Holy Ghost."

Baptism: Cleaning the Slate

Again, I will preface this chapter on baptism by saying that I will not divide denominations by arguing for or against specific baptism practices. The point of this chapter is to explain what this act means in the Mormon Church relative to mainstream Christianity, and how that impacts members and changes the intentions of the Bible.

My understanding of baptism growing up was very different than my understanding now. Everything prior to my eighth birthday did not count. I believed that my baptism was a literal cleansing of my sins, and after my baptism I was completely sinless, starting again at zero. I would relate the Holy Ghost in the Mormon Church with a conscience. Once I received the laying on of hands for the gift of the Holy Spirit, it would help me determine between right and wrong. "Repent and be baptized in the name of Jesus Christ, according to the holy commandment, for the remission of sins; And whoso doeth this shall receive the gift of the Holy Ghost, by the laying on of the hands of the elders of the church" Doctrine & Covenants 43:13-14.

From that point forward, I was accountable for my actions and had to repent for every sin I committed. "For all men must repent and be baptized, and not only men, but women, and children who have arrived at the years of accountability. And now, after that you have received this, you must keep my commandments in all things" Doctrine & Covenants 18:42.

Let's start with the topic of baptism in the Mormon Church. Sacraments are a hot topic in any church, and in fact, many times the sacraments are what differentiate one Christian denomination from another – not the core of our beliefs. It is impossible for me to discuss these sacraments without being at least a little influenced by my own beliefs.

To give you my perspective before going further, I would say that of course I believe that baptism is important and all Christians should be baptized. However, I do not believe that it is absolutely necessary to be baptized to go to heaven. After all, what is the point of grace when it is not truly grace? We are saved by grace through faith alone. If baptism was mandatory for entry into heaven, then it would be a requirement of an act – which the Bible states several times are not required. Is it important? Absolutely. Is it a requirement for entry into heaven? No.

There are some Christian Churches who will simply bless infants and wait for them to make the decision to become baptized, and others who will strongly encourage infant baptism. Within the Mormon Church, blessings will be given to infants in lieu of baptism. "Every member of the church of Christ having children is to bring them unto the elders before the church, who are to lay their hands upon them in the name of Jesus Christ, and bless them in his name" Doctrine & Covenants 20:70. I was blessed as a child, as were my siblings.

The Doctrine & Covenants is very specific on how baptisms are to be performed. "The person who is called of God and has authority from Jesus Christ to baptize, shall go down into the water with the person who has presented himself or herself for baptism, and shall say, calling him or her by her name: Having been commissioned of Jesus Christ, I baptize you in the name of the Father, and of the Son, and of the Holy Ghost. Amen. Then he shall immerse him or her in the water, and come forth again out of the water" Doctrine & Covenants 20:73-74. As you can see, this is exactly how my father baptized me and exactly as the Mormon scripture commands.

Unlike some mainstream Christian churches, the LDS church is very, very specific about the age of accountability and the risks of not conforming to their age restrictions. "And again, inasmuch as parents have children in Zion, or in any of her stakes which are organized, that teach them not to understand the doctrine of repentance, faith in Christ the Son of the living God, and of baptism and the gift of the Holy Ghost by the laying on of hands, when eight years old, the sin be upon the heads of the parents…And their children shall be baptized for the remission of their sins when eight years old, and receive the laying on of the hands. And they shall also teach their children to pray, and to walk uprightly before the Lord" Doctrine & Covenants 68:25-28. Many parents, mine included, within the Mormon Church are very strict with these responsibilities. It would risk their salvation if they did not take them seriously.

We mentioned earlier that the Bible is silent on the issue of children and their Salvation. God is a merciful God, but the Bible does not directly address the salvation of un-baptized children. The Mormon scriptures, on the other hand, do make a statement regarding the salvation of children.

"But behold, I say unto you, that the little children are redeemed from the foundation of the world through mine Only Begotten; wherefore, they cannot sin, for the power is not given unto Satan to tempt little children, until they begin to become accountable before me" Doctrine & Covenants 29:46-47.

This belief in the innocence of children stems back to the lack of original sin, and the fact that Mormons do not believe in original sin. As stated here, it is actually not until you are baptized and receive the Holy Spirit that you actually become accountable for your actions and Satan can influence your actions. I find it interesting that God would have the innate ability to protect young children, but not have the capacity to protect those who are older. Why is Satan given power over adults and not children? Interesting concept. Not in the Bible.

Laying on of Hands for the Holy Spirit

The laying on of hands is also an interesting matter. Mainstream Christians believe that it is simply the baptism itself that stirs faith in the heart of the baptized individual. However, Mormons believe that it is through the laying on of hands that the Holy Spirit is received. There is nothing wrong with the laying on of hands, as it is not an uncommon tradition throughout Christianity.

Just as I said earlier this chapter, I sat in a chair and the elders of the church placed their hands on my head to bless me with the Holy Spirit. The laying on of hands is also how people are confirmed into their positions within the Mormon Church. If you are called to be the bishop of the church, or have a specific position, this is confirmed through the laying on of hands.

This follows in line with the tenth article of Mormon faith, "We believe that a man must be called of God, by prophecy, and by the laying on of hands by those who are in authority, to preach the Gospel and administer in the ordinances thereof."

Since God and Jesus are two separate individuals within the Mormon Church, there is also a distinction in the Mormon faith between who cares for the children. Insomuch as Jesus said, "Suffer the little children and let them come unto me" Luke 18:16, he also took possession of their care, in a way. "Fear not, little children, for you are mine, and I have overcome the world, and you are of them that my Father hath given me; and none of them that my Father hath given me shall be lost" Doctrine & Covenants 50:41-42.

In this way Jesus, again separate from God, is seen as the caretaker of the children of this earth who are taken before their age of accountability. The question that comes up for me is, if children belong to Jesus and are under the care of Jesus, at what point does Jesus give them back to God? When they turn eight years old?

The silence of the Bible on the subject of infant death and the death of a child is difficult for many, as our human nature wants answers to these puzzling and often deeply emotional questions. While the Bible remains silent on this subject, the Mormon Church has added to the sphere of knowledge presented in Bible to create answers for those questions that for the rest of Christianity remain somewhat unanswered. And while providing answers may make us all feel better in our darkest moments, one must really ask if these are just words or if they are real truth.

It is important to understand original sin, grace and salvation before you can thoroughly understand the Mormon view on baptism. Mormons believe that baptism is necessary for access to the celestial kingdom of heaven, the highest eternity they can aspire to. In this realm of heaven, they can attain God-like powers and dwell with God and Jesus – again separate beings – on a regular basis. Understanding these aspects of Mormonism will make sense of one of the greatest controversies between Mormonism and mainstream Christianity, and that is baptisms for the dead.

Baptisms for the Dead

Throughout the history of time, there are people who have lived on the earth who have not heard of Jesus Christ and were not baptized, or did not understand the importance of baptism. Mormons also maintain that some people were baptized by a person who was not of the authority to perform the baptism (men in the Mormon priesthood). They believe that as a result of these people being unable to be baptized, God has authorized baptism by proxy. You may recall that the second level of heaven can be accessed by those who have chosen to accept Christ while they are in the spirit world, before the Second Coming.

A living person in the Mormon Church can be baptized on behalf of others who have died. Most often people are baptized for the deceased members of their families, in hopes that they will be able to provide salvation to their family members. You may recognize that many Mormons have a huge interest in their genealogy, and that the church has vast resources dedicated to genealogical research. This is primarily due to their vested interests in providing salvation to all family members by performing baptisms on their behalf.

The thought of baptisms by proxy instills quite a bit of fear in the mainstream Christian community. People opposed to Mormonism do not want baptisms performed on their behalf, as they do not share their beliefs with the LDS church. However, it should be noted that Mormons believe that these baptisms by proxy are not done against the will of the deceased individual. Mormons believe that when people die, they go to the spirit world. Before the second coming of Jesus, people in the spirit world have the ability to accept and follow the teachings of Jesus and accept the Mormon faith.

In the New Testament, Paul writes in 1 Corinthians 15:29, "Else what shall they do which are baptized for the dead, if the dead rise not at all? Why are they then baptized for the dead?" It is specific Biblical reference to baptisms for the dead that Mormons feel called out to a requirement from God to perform baptisms for the dead. They believe that this ability to perform such baptisms was restored to the Mormon Church when Joseph Smith received his priesthood.

Since this is the Mormon Church's primary citation for baptisms for the dead, I would like to make a few distinctions. In Romans 6:4 is says "Therefore we are buried with him by baptism into death: that like as Christ was raised up from the dead by the glory of the Father, even so we should walk in newness of life." Baptism is an acknowledgment of our sins, and a figurative way of entering a grave of water, and emerging from that grave just as Christ conquered death through his resurrection. In this way, baptism is also a similitude of the resurrection of Christ. "For we have been planted together in the likeness of his death, we shall be also in the likeness of his resurrection" Romans 6:5. Just as Christ emerged from the grave and was resurrected, we too emerge from the grave and will be resurrected.

The points made in 1 Corinthians 15:29 are not to condone the baptisms of those who have died. Instead, the point is that those who are baptized in Christ are proof of the resurrection and hope for those who have died. There is also a bit of confusion regarding Biblical translation here of the word 'for'. Here the Greek word 'huper' is translated into the word 'for', but 'huper' has many meanings (such as 'over' or 'for the hope of' or 'above') and the context can change the meaning of this word. In this case, 1 Corinthians 15:29 is not actually saying that you should be baptized in place of the dead.

Rather, it is saying that that you should be baptized for the hope of the dead. In this case, the hope of the dead is resurrection, which is symbolized through baptism.

These baptisms for the dead are performed exclusively at Mormon temples. In Doctrine & Covenants 124, God commanded the Mormon people to build temples to do this work because none of their facilities were good enough to suit this purpose yet. "For a baptismal font there is not upon the earth, that they, my saints, may be baptized for those who are dead – for this ordinance belongeth to my house, and cannot be acceptable to me, only in the days of your poverty, wherein ye are not able to build a house unto me" Doctrine & Covenants 124:29-30.

Performing baptisms for the dead is not optional in the LDS church. In fact, this is another necessary step for salvation. "For therein are the keys of the holy priesthood ordained, that you may receive honor and glory" Doctrine & Covenants 124:34. Baptisms for the dead are a requirement for those seeking the glory of the celestial kingdom of heaven.

Sealing Your Family

Genealogy is my grandmother's favorite pastime. She and my grandfather have gone all around the country finding lists, documents, newspapers, obituaries and graves of our ancestors, in an effort to document and record the lives of these people. These genealogical records are imperative not only to the Mormon person's salvation, but to the salvation of their ancestors.

On April 3, 1836, Mormon history explains that the prophet Elijah came to Joseph Smith and his companion Oliver Cowdery at the temple they had built. On that day, it was recorded that the prophet Elijah gave them the power of the priesthood, which would allow them to seal families together. If you ever visit a Mormon home, you may see plaques or paintings that say 'for time and all eternity' or 'families can be together forever'.

Mormons believe that through this priesthood power that Elijah restored to the earth, their families can be sealed together forever. In the Book of Mormon, Malachi 4:5-6 there was a prophecy, "Behold, I will send you Elijah the prophet before the coming of the great and dreadful day of the Lord: And he shall turn the heart of the fathers to the children and the heart of the children to their fathers, lest I come and smite the earth with a curse."

Mormons maintain that this prophecy was fulfilled when Joseph Smith and Oliver Cowdery received this revelation and priesthood power from Elijah. It is comical to me that you can write a tale of prophecy in the Book of Mormon and subsequently fulfill your own prophecy by claiming revelations in your own Doctrine & Covenants. Yes, the prophecy you made up in one book *you* wrote came true in another book *you* wrote. What a surprise!

Mormons believe that they are continuing to fulfill this prophecy by searching for their ancestors and documenting their findings. Doctrine & Covenants 128:18 says, "I might have rendered a plainer translation to this, but it is sufficiently plain to suit my purpose as it stands. It is sufficient to know, in this case, that the earth will be smitten with a curse unless there is a welding link of some kind or other between the fathers and the children, upon some subject or other – and behold what is that subject? It is the baptism for the dead…"

There are sacred temple ordinances that Mormons perform on behalf of their dead ancestors, and those are what they consider the welding link between fathers and their children. Mormons believe that if they perform these works on behalf of their ancestors, they will become saviors on Mount Zion for their family members in the last days, referencing the Bible "And saviours shall come up on mount Zion to judge the mount of Esau; and the kingdom shall be the Lord's" Obadiah 1:21.

Genealogical records are so important in the Mormon Church because as we mentioned regarding baptisms for the dead, both the salvation of the living and the dead are dependent upon that act. It is imperative that Mormons find their ancestors and are baptized on their behalf, to ensure that their ancestors' salvation may be possible. The performance of the act of baptism for the dead is also a requirement for their own salvation, and is a necessary act to enter the highest level of heaven.

Extensive records are kept in the church archives, for the purpose of permitting as many baptisms for the dead as possible. Mormons view this genealogical research as a responsibility both to their families and to God.

Of course, all baptisms for the dead must be recorded in the records of the church, or they do not count with God.

"Verily, thus saith the Lord unto you concerning your dead: When any of you are baptized for your dead, let there be a recorder, and let him be eye-witness of your baptisms; let him hear with his ears, that he may testify of a truth, saith the Lord; That in all your recordings it may be recorded in heaven; whatsoever you bind on earth, may be bound in heaven; whatsoever you loose on earth, may be loosed in heaven…and again, let all records be had in order, that they may be put in the archives of my holy temple, to be held in remembrance from generation to generations, saith the Lord of Hosts" Doctrine & Covenants 127:6-9.

Mormons believe that if they do not write these things into their records, God will not have them recorded in heaven and their family members will not gain salvation. For that reason, the record keeping in the LDS church is incredibly meticulous.

Mormons often site these records as being the books that John was referencing in Revelation 20:12, "And I saw the dead, small and great, stand before God; and the books were opened; and another book was opened, which was the book of life; and the dead were judged out of those thing which were written in the books, according to their works."

Mormons believe that the records they are keeping on this earth are those books which will be opened by God in heaven, and the book of life is the record that is kept in heaven. These two books should match, as they believe that what is written on earth is also written in heaven.

The dead who were baptized by proxy will also be judged by these books, "For out of the books shall your dead be judged, according to their own works, whether they themselves have attended to the ordinances in their own propria persona, or by the means of their own agents, according to the ordinances which God has prepared for their salvation from before the foundation of the world, according to the records which they have kept concerning their dead" Doctrine & Covenants 128:8.

Sacraments

Sacrament is also a very particular memory for me. We never called it communion. I remember hearing people use the term communion and I had no idea what they were talking about. This term can be a bit confusing in Mormonism because what some people would refer to as 'mass' or 'sermons' would also be what we called Sacrament. We took the Sacrament during Sacrament – confusing, right? We would sit in the pews and the priests and teachers would go up to the front of the congregation, on what I would call the stage.

Usually on one side there was an area where the priests and teachers would set up the Sacrament service. They would take pieces of bread and break them up with their hands, putting them into little baskets.

They would then say the prayer, "O God, the Eternal Father, we ask to sanctify this bread to the souls of all those who partake of it, that they may eat it in the remembrance of the body of thy Son, and witness unto thee, O God, the Eternal Father, that they are willing to take upon them the name of thy Son, and always remember him and keep his commandments which he has given them; that they may always have his Spirit to be with them. Amen" Doctrine & Covenants 20:77.

The priests had to memorize this prayer, and say it into the microphone. After they said it, they would look at the Bishop. If they made no errors, it was acceptable to move on. If they made any errors, they would have to continue saying the prayer again until they got it correct. The deacons would then pass out the bread as the body of Christ.

Then the deacons would come back to drop off the empty baskets, and take the water trays. They would say another prayer, "O God, the Eternal Father, we ask the in the name of thy Son, Jesus Christ, to bless and sanctify this wine to the souls of all those who drink of it, that they may do it in remembrance of the blood of thy Son, which was shed for them; that they may witness unto thee, O God, the Eternal Father, that they do always remember him, that they may have his Spirit to be with them. Amen" Doctrine & Covenants 20:79. The deacons would then pass out the water as the blood of Christ, since we could not drink wine or even grape juice.

We took the Sacrament every single Sunday, without exception. Just water and bread. It was a completely foreign concept to me until my recent footsteps into Christianity that people had these unleavened bread discs and wine with what they called communion. We weren't allowed to take a sip of alcohol, so surely it was unacceptable to partake of wine in God's house.

"For, behold, I say unto you, that it mattereth not what ye shall eat or what ye shall drink when ye partake of the sacrament, if it so be that ye do it with an eye single to my glory – remembering unto the Father my body which was laid down for you, and my blood which was shed for the remission of your sins. Wherefore, a commandment I give unto you, that you shall not purchase wine neither strong drink of your enemies" Doctrine & Covenants 27:2-3.

On one hand, it is unimportant what is partaken of as long as it is done to glorify God. On the other, it is important because Mormons believe that they are commanded not to drink alcohol.

Baptism, the laying on of hands and Sacraments are all crucial not only to salvation in the Mormon faith, but also to the day-to-day happenings of the Mormon Church. All of their beliefs addressed earlier in this book are tied into these three traditions, each intertwined and influencing the other.

The greatest and most controversial of these rituals is baptism for the dead, being an unaccepted practice throughout mainstream Christianity. It is my belief that the changes addressed in the Doctrine & Covenants on these issues are yet another example of adding to the original intent and meaning of the Bible. This will become even more apparent in the next chapter.

RESTATEMENTS, REVISED EXPLANATIONS & CONTRADICTIONS

As you may have noticed from the Revelations and Mormon Doctrine I have outlined in this book, there are many places where Mormonism makes a point to 'clarify' those subjects that are silent in the Bible.

As mainstream Christians understand, there are some subjects that God did not elaborate on in the Bible. For example, what happens to children when they die, or what we will experience upon death? There are keys and hints, but these details are not discussed outright.

Mormonism really focuses on what happens after death in relation to the works we performed within our lives on earth. Since they view this life as a test and not a gift, it alters the meaning of their Christianity. They are no longer doing good works as a result of their relationship with God, they are actually performing good works in an attempt to promote their own exaltation and eventually become God-like themselves. Big, big difference.

Throughout this book, I have cited several revised explanations offered by the Mormon Doctrine. However, I believe that it is important to demonstrate a few more places in Mormon doctrine where the intent of the Bible is altered, including several 'question and answer' sessions that Joseph Smith said he had with God. No joke, they are actually written in the Doctrine & Covenants in Q&A format.

Typically, I have not gone chapter and verse, citing entire sections of the Doctrine & Covenants. However, I believe that there are specific sections of the Doctrine & Covenants that explain the thought process of Joseph Smith, and better explain the establishment of the Mormon Church through revelations. To witness to a person of Mormon faith, you must first understand the manner in which they have been taught. Mormonism openly accepts and encourages revelations. As you have already seen in this book, some of these revelations can and have altered the meaning or intent of some Biblical verses entirely. It is important to understand that the Mormon view of the Bible differs from mainstream Christianity, and they have used their own scriptures to fill in for areas of the Bible where God remains silent on certain subjects.

Reinterpretation through Revelation

One very blatant example of these revised explanations is seen in Doctrine & Covenants, Chapter 77. In this chapter, Joseph Smith is reinterpreting the Bible (on a side note, Joseph's Smith's version of the Bible is not really used in the LDS Church today, and the King James Version is readily accepted as well – go figure). Upon his interpretations, he asked God some questions about the Bible that he felt were unclear to him.

Through divine revelations, Mormons believe that Joseph received the answers he was seeking. This is one of the few chapters in the Doctrine & Covenants that is actually in a 'Q&A' type format. This Q&A session is regarding the Book of Revelations. In my opinion, Revelations is one of the most complicated and difficult sections in the Bible to comprehend, containing many explanations that are in all likelihood, intended to be beyond our complete comprehension.

Bible verse in Question – Revelations 4:6, "And before the throne there was a sea of glass like unto crystal; and in the midst of the throne, and round about the throne, were four beasts full of eyes before and behind."

Question One: What is the sea of glass spoken of by John, 4th chapter, and 6th verse of the Revelation?" Doctrine & Covenants 77:1.

God's Answer: "The earth, in its sanctified, immortal and eternal state" Doctrine & Covenants 77:1.

Question Two: "What are we to understand by the four beasts, spoken of in the same verse?" Doctrine & Covenants 77:2.

God's Answer: "They are figurative expressions, used by the Revelator, John, in describing heaven, the paradise of God, the happiness of man, and of beasts, and of creeping things, and of the fowls of the air, that which is spiritual being in the likeness of that which is temporal; and that which is temporal in the likeness of that which is spiritual; and the spirit of man in the likeness of his person, as also the spirit of the beast, and every other creature which God has created" Doctrine & Covenants 77:2.

Question Three: "Are the four beasts limited to individual beasts, or do they represent classes or orders?" Doctrine & Covenants 77:3.

God's Answer: "They are limited to four individual beasts, which were shown to John, to represent the glory of the classes of beings in their destined order or sphere of creation, in the enjoyment of their eternal felicity" Doctrine & Covenants 77:3.

Bible verse in Question – Revelations 4:7-8, "And the first beast was like a lion, and the second beast like a calf, and the third beast had a face as a man, and the fourth beast was like a flying eagle. And the four beasts had each of them six wings about him; and they were full of eyes within: and they rest not day and night, saying, Holy, holy, holy, Lord God Almighty, which was, and is, and is to come."

Question: "What are we to understand by the eyes and wings, which the beasts had?" Doctrine & Covenants 77:4.

God's Answer: "Their eyes are a representation of light and knowledge, that is, they are full of knowledge, and their wings are a representation of power, to move, to act, etc" Doctrine & Covenants 77:4.

Bible verse in Question – Revelations 4:10, "The four and twenty elders fall down before him that sat on the throne, and worship him that liveth forever and ever, and cast their crowns before the throne, saying, Thou art worth, O Lord, to receive glory and honour and power: for thou has created all things, and for thy pleasure they are and were created."

Question: "What are we to understand by the four and twenty elders, spoken of by John?" Doctrine & Covenants 77:5.

Answer: We are to understand that these elders whom John saw, were elders who had been faithful in the work of the ministry and were dead, who belonged to the seven churches, and were then in the paradise of God" Doctrine & Covenants 77:5

Bible verse in Question – Revelations 5:1, ""And I saw in the right hand of him that sat on the throne a book written within and on the backside, sealed with seven seals."

Question: "What are we to understand by the book which John saw, which was sealed on the back with seven seals? What are we to understand by the seven seals with which it was sealed?" Doctrine & Covenants 77:6-7.

God's Answer: "We are to understand that it contains the revealed will, mysteries, and the works of God; the hidden things of his economy concerning this earth during the seven thousand years of its continuance, or its temporal existence. We are to understand that the first seal contains the things of the first thousand years, and the second also of the second thousand years, and so on until the seventh." Doctrine & Covenants 77:6-7.

Bible verse in Question – Revelations 7:1, "And after these things I saw four angels standing on the four corners of the earth, holding the four winds of the earth, that the wind should not blow on the earth, nor on the sea, nor on any tree."

Question: "What are we to understand by the four angels, spoken of in the 7th chapter and 1st verse of Revelation?" Doctrine & Covenants 77:8

God's Answer: "We are to understand that they are four angels sent forth from God, to whom is given power over the four parts of the earth, to save life and to destroy; these are they who have the everlasting gospel to commit to every nation, kindred, tongue, and people; having the power to shut up the heavens, to seal up unto life, or to cast down to the regions of darkness" Doctrine & Covenants 77:8

Bible verse in Question – Revelations 7:2, "And I saw another angel ascending from the east, having the seal of the living God: and he cried with a loud voice to the four angels, to whom it was given to hurt the earth and sea"

Question: "What are we to understand by the angel ascending from the east, Revelation 7th chapter and 2nd verse? What time are the things spoken of in this chapter to be accomplished?" Doctrine & Covenants 77:9-10

Answer: "We are to understand that the angel ascending from the east is he to whom is given the seal of the living God over the twelve tribes of Israel; wherefore he crieth unto the four angels having the everlasting gospel, saying: Hurt not the earth, neither the sea, nor the trees, till we have sealed the servants of our God in their foreheads. And if you will receive it, this is Elias which was to come gather together the tribes of Israel and restore all things. They are to be accomplished in the sixth thousand years, or the opening of the sixth seal." Doctrine & Covenants 77:9-10

Bible verse in Question – Revelations 7:4-11, "And heard the number of them which were sealed: and there were sealed an hundred and forty and four thousand of all the tribes of the children of Israel…After this I beheld, and, lo, a great multitude which no man could number, of all nations, and kindreds, and people, and tongues, stood before the throne, and before the Lamb, clothed with white robes, and palms on their hands; And cried with a loud voice saying, Salvation to our God which sitteth upon the throne, and unto the Lamb. And all the angles stood round about the throne, and about the elders and the four beasts, and fell before the throne on their faces, and worshipped God."

Question: "What are we to understand by sealing the one hundred and forty-four thousand, out of all the tribes of Israel – twelve thousand out of every tribe?" Doctrine & Covenants 77:11.

God's Answer: "We are to understand that those who are sealed are high priests, ordained unto the holy order of God, to administer the everlasting gospel; for they are they who are ordained out of every nation, kindred, tongue and people, by the angels to whom is given power over the nations of the earth, to bring as many will come to the church of the Firstborn" Doctrine & Covenants 77:11.

Bible verse in Question – Revelations, all of Chapter 8; in summary, this chapter explains that when Jesus opened the seventh seal, silence fell for half an hour. Then seven angels appeared with seven trumpets, each of the trumpets being blown, individually resulting in a third of several different devastations to the earth.

Question: "What are we to understand by the sounding of the trumpets, mentioned in the 8th chapter of Revelation?" Doctrine & Covenants 77:12

Answer: "We are to understand that as God made the world in six days, and on the seventh day he finished his work, and sanctified it, also formed man out of the dust of the earth, even so, in the beginning of the seventh thousand years will the Lord God sanctify the earth, and complete the salvation of man, and judge all things, and shall redeem all things, except that which he hath not put into his power, when he shall have sealed all things, unto the end of all things; and the sounding of the trumpets of the seven angels are the preparing and finishing of his work, in the beginning of the seventh thousand years – the preparing of the way before the time of his coming."

Bible verse in Question – Revelations, all of Chapter 9; in summary, the ninth chapter of Revelations is a continuation of the eighth, explaining the actions upon the trumpets of the fifth and sixth angels.

Question: "When are the things to be accomplished, which are written in the 9th chapter of Revelation?"

Answer: "They are to be accomplished after the opening of the seventh seal, before the coming of Christ" Doctrine & Covenants 77:13.

Bible verse in Question – Revelations, all of Chapter 10; in summary, John takes a scroll from another angel and is told to eat the scroll, and John did.

Question: "What are we to understand by the little book which was eaten by John, as mentioned in the 10th chapter of Revelation?" Doctrine & Covenants 77:14.

Answer: "We are to understand that it was a mission, and an ordinance, for him to gather the tribes of Israel; behold, this is Elias, who, as it is written, must come and restore all things" Doctrine & Covenants 77:14.

Bible verse in Question – Revelations, all of Chapter 11; in summary, This eleventh chapter speaks of two prophets, or witnesses, that will prophesy in the last days of the earth.

Question: "What is to be understood by the two witnesses, in the eleventh chapter of Revelation?" Doctrine & Covenants 77:15.

Answer: "They are two prophets that are to be raised up to the Jewish nation in the last days, at the time of the restoration, and to prophesy to the Jews after they are gathered and have built the city of Jerusalem in the land of their fathers" Doctrine & Covenants 77:15.

Okay, so what's that point of all of this? Why would I go verse by verse through the entire 77th chapter of Doctrine & Covenants, a book that mainstream Christians don't even believe to be true? Because Mormons believe it is true. There are few places where the perversions of the Biblical texts are as transparent as in these question and answer sessions with God. I would equate this chapter in the Doctrine & Covenants with a sales pitch (I work sales, so I can do that).

Let's say you're selling a product called Salvation. You don't have a lot of references, records or proof to back up what you are saying, but you do have a pretty sweet brochure. No matter what question you ask, I can warp the evidence and records that I do have to promote my product. I can take a reference like the Bible and through revelations I can make it say what I want it to say, and create correlations between the existing text and the text I made up. Mormons are sold on the ideology that through revelations, we can say the things that we think the Bible meant to say.

The reason I have gone through all fifteen questions asked by Joseph to God in Doctrine & Covenants chapter 77 is to illustrate the way that the Mormon Church purveys and alters the information presented to their people through revelations.

The actual book of Revelations is complex, with quite descriptive but non-specific details related to things that will occur at the end of days. Physical revelations in the Mormon Church are not considered opinions, but rather divine facts, inspired by God. I find it strange that God would not be specific in the Bible, but would later choose to reveal greater secrets – which are angled towards the beliefs of the LDS church.

Why would God have kept such secrets of Salvation? These revelations add to the words and intent of the Bible. If the Bible is the inerrant Word of God, I would say that God said exactly what he wanted to say in the Book of Revelations, and nothing more.

The Book of Revelations is not the only Biblical book to spawn and line of questioning from Joseph Smith. The book of Isaiah also causes some confusion, and leads to another Question & Answer session with God.

Reinterpreting Isaiah

Bible verse in Question – Isaiah 11:1-5; "And there shall come forth a rod out of the stem of Jesse, and a Branch shall grow out of his roots: And the spirit of the Lord shall rest upon him, the spirit of wisdom and understanding, the spirit of counsel and might, the spirit of knowledge and of the fear of the Lord; And shall make him of quick understanding in the fear of the Lord: and he shall not judge after the sight of his eyes, neither reprove after the hearing of his ears; But with righteousness shall he judge the poor, and reprove with equity for the meek of the earth: and he shall smite the earth with the rod of his mouth, and with the breath of his lips shall he slay the wicked. And righteousness shall be the girdle of his loins, and faithfulness the girdle of his reins."

Question One: "Who is the Stem of Jesse spoken in the 1st, 2nd, 3rd, 4th and 5th versus of the 1th chapter if Isaiah?" Doctrine & Covenants 113:1.

Answer: "Verily thus saith the Lord: it is Christ" Doctrine & Covenants 113:2.

Question Two: "What is the rod spoken of in the first verse of the 11th chapter of Isaiah that should come from the stem of Jesse?"

Answer: "Behold, thus saith the Lord: It is a servant in the hands of Christ, who is partly a descendant of Jesse as well as of Ephraim, or of the house of Joseph, on whom there is laid much power" Doctrine & Covenants 113:4.

Bible verse in Question – Isaiah 11:10-11; "And in that day there shall be a root of Jesse, which shall stand for an ensign of the people; to it shall the Gentiles seek; and his rest shall be glorious. And it shall come to pass in that day, that the Lord shall set his hand again the second time to recover the remnant of his people, which shall be left, from Assyria, and from Egypt, and from Pathros, and from Cush, and from Elam, and from Shinar, and from Hamath, and from the islands of the sea."

Question One: "What is the root of Jesse spoken of in the 10th verse of the 11th chapter?" Doctrine & Covenants 113:5.

Answer: "Behold, thus saith the Lord, it is a descendant of Jesse, as well as of Joseph, unto whom rightly belongs the priesthood, and the keys of the kingdom, for an ensign, and for the gathering of my people in the last days" Doctrine & Covenants 113:6.

Question Two: "What is meant by the command in Isaiah, 52nd chapter, 1st verse, which saith: Put on thy strength, O Zion – and what people had Isaiah reference to?" Doctrine & Covenants 113:7.

Answer: "He had reference to those whom God should call in the last days, who should hold the power of priesthood to bring again Zion, and the redemption of Israel; and to put on her strength is to put on the authority of the priesthood, which she, Zion, has a right to by lineage; also to return to the power which she had lost" Doctrine & Covenants 113:8.

Reinterpreting 1 Corinthians

Bible verse in Question –1 Corinthian, all of Chapter 7; "But to the rest speak I, not the Lord: If any brother hath a wife that believeth not, and she be pleased to dwell with him, let him not put her away. And the woman which hath a husband that believeth not, and if he be pleased to dwell with her, let her not leave him. For the unbelieving husband is sanctified by the wife and the unbelieving wife is sanctified by the husband: else were your children unclean; but now are they holy...Is any man called being circumcised? Let him not become uncircumcised. Is any called in uncircumcision? Let him not be circumcised. Circumcision is nothing, and uncircumcision is nothing, but the keeping of the commandments of God." 1 Corinthian 7:12-19

These verses are discussing the holiness provided to spouses through their partners who believe in Christ, as we are all called to live the life that God intended us to live. As such, if a man is circumcised or uncircumcised at the time of his calling, it does not make any difference as long as he is following the commandments of God in his life. The Mormon faith and doctrine point to this verse and make an attempt to further explain this verse through revelations.

Revelation to Joseph Smith: "Now, in the days of the apostles the law of circumcision was had among all the Jews who believed not the gospel of Jesus Christ. And it came to pass that there arose a great contention among the people concerning the law of circumcision, for the unbelieving husband was desirous that his children should be circumcised and become subject to the Law of Moses, which law was fulfilled. And it came to pass that the children, being brought up in subjection to the Law of Moses, gave heed to the traditions of their fathers and believed not in the gospel of Christ, wherein they became unholy. Wherefore, for this cause the apostle wrote unto the church, giving unto them a commandment, not of the Lord, but of himself, that a believer should not be united to an unbeliever, except the law of Moses should be done away among them, that their children might remain without circumcision; and that the tradition might be done away, which saith that little children are unholy; for it was had among the Jews; But little children are holy, being sanctified through the atonement of Jesus Christ; and this is what the scriptures mean" Doctrine & Covenants 74: 2-7.

While this passage in the Mormon doctrine is a bit long, it is also very illustrative of the conclusions drawn by the Mormon faith through their revelations. Rather than taking this Biblical reference to circumcision at face value, Mormons actually deduce from this text that the Bible 'means' that the children are holy and without sin.

This would mean that there is no such thing as original sin, which in my opinion is not what this Bible passage is saying at all. Changing the intentions of this text is basically saying that original sin does not exist, which in turn changes grace. Interesting change. Not in the Bible.

Reinterpreting the Bible – Did he say baptisms for the dead?

Bible Verse in Question – Matthew 16:18-19 states, "And I say also unto thee, that thou art Peter, and upon this rock I will build my church; and the gates of hell shall not prevail against it. And I will give unto thee the keys of the kingdom of heaven: and whatsoever thou shalt bind on earth shall be bound in heaven: and whatsoever thou shalt loose on earth shall be loosed in heaven."

Extremely interesting text related to the Mormon belief in baptism for the dead is also provided through revelations documented in Doctrine & Covenants chapter 128. In Doctrine & Covenants 128:10, Joseph received a revelation from God regarding baptisms for the dead and referenced Matthew 16:18-19 as a precedent for these works. Mormons maintain that the keys referenced in the Book of Matthew are actually the keys of the Mormon priesthood.

<u>Revelation to Joseph Smith</u>: "Now the great and grand secret of the whole matter, and the summum bonum of the whole subject that is lying before us, consists in obtaining the powers of the Holy Priesthood. For him to whom these keys are given there is no difficulty in obtaining a knowledge of facts in relation to the salvation of the children of men, both as well for the dead as for the living" Doctrine & Covenants 128:11.

The term *summum bonum* here is Latin, meaning the 'highest good'. This phrase is often used to describe an ultimate life or end which we are all, as humans, supposed to desire and pursue.

These verses are explaining that the ultimate end to all men should be obtaining the Mormon priesthood powers, which will provide him with an understanding of salvation for the living and the dead.

Bible Verse in Question – 1 Corinthians 15:46-48; "Howbeit that was not first which is spiritual, but that which is natural; and afterward that which is spiritual. The first man is of the earth, earthy: the second man is the Lord from heaven. As is the earthy, such are they also that are earthy: and as is the heavenly, such are they also that are heavenly".

This verse is explaining that your natural, physical body comes first, and then the spiritual. It is interesting that they site this passage for their own reference regarding baptism for the dead, because it is actually contradictory to the Mormon belief that people existed in heaven as spirits before coming to earth and being tested, and proving ourselves in front of God. If we are not spirits until we are earthly beings, then there cannot be a spirit heaven as they speak of. However, that is not how Joseph Smith interprets this.

Revelation to Joseph Smith: "Consequently, the baptismal font was instituted as a similitude of the grave, and was commanded to be in a place underneath where the living are wont to assemble, to show forth the living and the dead, and that all things may have their likeness, and that they may accord one with another – that which is earthly confirming to that which is heavenly, as Paul hath declared, 1 Corinthians 15:46-48…and as are the records on earth in relation to your dead, which are truly made out, so also are the records in heaven. This, therefore, is the sealing and binding power, and in one sense of the word, the keys of the kingdom, which consist in the key of knowledge" Doctrine & Covenants 128:13-14.

Again, Joseph Smith ties bible verses to unrelated concepts. While the Bible is talking about the earthly being first and the spiritual second, Joseph Smith is talking about the records in relation to those who have passed.

While these are seemingly unrelated, Joseph uses this verse to further the thought that those records that are made on earth must be the same as those kept in heaven. From my perspective, these may be similar thoughts but I do not think that this is what Paul had in mind.

Bible Verse in Question #1 – 1 Peter 3:18-20; "For Christ also hath once suffered for sins, the just for the unjust, that he might bring us to God, being put to death in the flesh, but quickened by the Spirit. By which also he went and preached unto the spirits in prison; which sometime were disobedient, when once the longsuffering of God waited in the days of Noah, while the ark was a preparing, wherein few, that is, eight souls were saved by water."

Bible Verse in Question #2 – 1 Peter 4:6; "For for this cause was the gospel preached also to them that are dead, that they might be judged according to men in the flesh, but live according to God in the spirit"

Bible Verse in Question #3 – 1 Corinthians 15:29; "Otherwise, what will they do who are baptized for the dead, if the dead do not rise at all? Why then are they baptized for the dead?"

Mormons use all three of these verses to promote their idea of baptisms for the dead, saying that it was a Biblical concept that was reinstated on the earth when Joseph received his priesthood.

Joseph received a series of revelations in response to these verses, regarding what happened to Jesus after his resurrection.

<u>Revelation to Joseph Smith</u>: "And I wondered at the words of Peter – wherein he said that the Son of God preached unto the spirits in prison, who sometime were disobedient, when once the long-suffering of God waited in the days of Noah – how it was possible for him to preach to those spirits and perform the necessary labor among them in so short a time. And as I wondered, my eyes were opened, and my understanding quickened, and I perceived that the Lord went not in person among the wicked and the disobedient who had rejected the truth, to teach them; But behold, from among the righteous, he organized his forces and appointed messengers, clothed with power and authority, and commissioned them to go forth and carry the light of the gospel to them that were in darkness, even to all the spirits of men; and thus was the gospel preached to the dead. And the chosen messengers went forth to declare the acceptable day of the Lord and proclaim liberty to the captives who were bound, even unto all who would repent of their sins and receive the gospel. Thus was the gospel preached to

those who had died in their sins, without a knowledge of the truth, or in transgression, having rejected the prophets" Doctrine & Covenants 138: 28-32.

This verse opens an incredibly unpopular argument in all Christians, a battle that I have faced personally and that my own friends have questioned strongly.

What happens to those people who do not receive the words of Jesus in their lifetimes? We do not want to believe that those people descend into hell, because that seems unfair to us. As this verse explains, the Mormon Church has created an answer to this burning question of theology. Mormons believe that sometime between Good Friday and Easter – sometime between the death and resurrection of Jesus – Christ went into the spirit world.

Mormons maintain that he made this journey to the spirit world so that those who rejected or did not hear the Word of God (and in this case, accept Mormonism) would have the opportunity to do so in the spirit world. But did the Bible say this anywhere? No.

Revelation from Joseph Smith: "These were taught faith in God, repentance from sin, vicarious baptisms for the remission of sins, the gift of the Holy Ghost by the laying on of hands, And all other principles of the gospel that were necessary for them to know in order to qualify themselves that they might be judged according to men in the flesh, but live according to God in the spirit…Thus was it made known that our Redeemer spent his time during his sojourn in the world of spirits, instructing and preparing the faithful spirits of the prophets who had testified of him in the flesh; that they might carry the message of redemption unto all the dead, unto whom he could not go personally, because of their rebellion and transgression, that they through the ministration of his servants might also hear his words…The dead who repent will be redeemed, through obedience to the ordinances of the house of God, and after they have paid the penalty of their transgressions, are they washed clean, shall receive a reward according to their works, for they are heirs of salvation" Doctrine & Covenants 138:33-59.

First, I will argue that these teachings are undeniably an addition to the original intention of the Bible. Take again, for example, 1 Peter 4:6.

This verse may be confusing if it is not read in context. There are five verses before verse six, which explain that Jesus will hold those who persecute his followers accountable for those actions upon their judgment day.

Looking at verses five and six together, "Who shall give account to him that is ready to judge the quick and the dead; For for this cause was the gospel preached also to them that are dead" 1Peter 4:5-6. If you take verse six in context with verse five, the Bible is actually saying that Christ will judge both those dead and alive. In my opinion, Peter is referencing those people who were alive when they heard the Word but are now deceased. Joseph Smith's interpretation of this text is simply just that – an interpretation – which was distorted from the original context of the verses to create a story that otherwise does not exist.

What's the Point?

Why, one may ask, would Mormons be so desperate to bring non-Mormons into their faith, if in the spirit world they can make the choice to just accept God later? What is the point of living a Godly life at all, and why are Mormons so fearful of any wrong-doing?

In the Book of Mormon, Alma 34:33-35, "And now, as I said unto you before, as ye have had so many witnesses, therefore, I beseech of you that ye do not procrastinate the day of your repentance until the end; for after this day of life, which is given us to prepare for eternity, behold if we do not improve our time while in this life, then cometh the night of darkness wherein there can be no labor performed…For behold, if ye have procrastinated the day of your repentance even until death, behold, ye have become subjected to the spirit of the devil, and he doth seal you his, therefore, the Spirit of the Lord hath withdrawn from you, and hath no place in you, and the devil hath all power over you; and this is the final state of the wicked."

Even in the Mormon's own doctrine, they cannot entirely make sense of their belief in having a choice in the spirit world. In the Book of Mormon, they are told that if they do not act and repent as they should, they will not be able to perform any labors to regain their salvation.

They are also saying that if they have not repented upon their death, they seal their fate in hell. If they truly believe the Book of Mormon, then how can they also believe in the Doctrine & Covenants, as these texts contradict each other?

This is reinforced again in 2 Nephi 9:24, "And if they will not repent and believe in his name, and be baptized in his name, and endure to the end, they must be damned; for the Lord God, the Holy One of Israel, has spoken it." How is it possible that in 2 Nephi, Mormons are commanded to repent, be baptized, and believe in God until the end of their life or be damned, if there is also a stipulation in the Doctrine & Covenants which permits non-believers to still gain access to heaven by proxy?

It is interesting to note that nowhere in the Mormon's own Book of Mormon is there any mention of baptisms for the dead or post-death selection of God for the receipt of salvation. The belief in baptisms for the dead and selection of salvation in a spirit world is a perversion of three biblical verses, and standing contradictions to biblical principles.

The Language of the Book of Mormon

One point was brought to my attention by a great Pastor, a point that I had not previously considered – is the literal language of the Mormon doctrine. All of the Mormon doctrine was written in old English, including the revelations of Joseph Smith in the Doctrine & Covenants which were not written until the early to mid-1800s.

At that time they no longer spoke old English. The King James Version of the Bible, the only version accepted by the Mormon Church, was first written in 1611. Naturally, language has greatly progressed over several hundred years and people have sought after versions of the Bible that are in modern English and much easier to read.

The King James Version of the Bible was extremely popular for many years, and was not displaced in popularity until Noah Webster (you may know him from his famous Webster's Dictionary) made a push to write the Bible in modern English. In fact, it was around the 1830's when Webster introduced the first modern translation of the Bible – right around the same time that Joseph Smith established the Mormon Church.

This first modern English version was actually quite unpopular as many still favored the Old English version King James Bible. It wasn't until the 1880's that the English Revised Version (ERV) finally became popular with mainstream Christianity. I would contend that Mormon Church's view in their eighth Article of Faith; "We believe the Bible to be the Word of God as far as it is translated correctly..." actually has more to do with the changing of the Bible from Old English to Modern English rather than the actual content of the Bible itself.

I also find it curious that the Book of Mormon was translated by Joseph Smith from some ancient American language (which as we mentioned earlier, has never really been established since no archaeological proof of such a civilization or language has been found) – into Old English.

Why would Joseph not translate the Book of Mormon into modern English, as was most likely spoken by Joseph Smith and the people of the time in which it was translated? Even further, why were all of the revelations that Joseph Smith had written into the Doctrine & Covenants in Old English? Does God only speak Old English? This concept is fascinating to me, as even today Mormons pray in an Old English format, saying things like "We thank thee for this day."

It simply does not make sense to me why all books and revelations would be translated into Old English, a format that is both difficult to understand and truly out-dated. My personal belief is that the goal behind writing the Book of Mormon in Old English, as well as the Doctrine & Covenants and the Pearl of Great Price, is to make those other Mormon doctrines sound more like the popular Bible of the time – the King James Version of the Bible.

As I have said before, I have used the King James Version of the Bible for all of my Biblical references. I have done this because that is the only Bible that the Mormon Church readily accepts to be accurate. New Bibles in modern English are being accepted by people all over the world for a reason.

During my childhood and even into my research for this book as an adult, I have found the King James Version of the Bible to be confusing. We do not speak in Old English, a language of four hundred years ago. In my research for this book I would find myself translating Biblical verses into other versions so I could understand the words being said, and then re-read the Old English version to try and understand it more clearly.

Part of the reason why the Mormon Doctrine, Bible included, is still in old English is for purposeful confusion, intentionally deceiving people and misleading them by passing off new doctrine as old and wise testimony. As a youth in the Mormon Church, all of our doctrine was in old English.

How could I possibly read and understand our scriptures without assistance? It was nearly impossible to read on my own, and it is still difficult to comprehend as an adult.

Mirror, Mirror, on the Wall

There are places in the Book of Mormon where the terminology purposefully mirrors the Bible. Again, I believe this is an attempt to make the Mormon doctrine to appear to be divine in nature, and similar to the popular Bible of the day. There are several places where the Book of Mormon literally restates phrases found in the Bible.

While some of the phrases are not prominent original thoughts, there is definitely a reproduction of thought and language between the two doctrines. The verbiage used in the Mormon doctrines is made to sound like that of the Bible, and as such leads people to believe it is from God rather than from man.

For example, in 1 Nephi 10:8, the end of this verse says, "and he is mightier than I, whose shoe's latchet I am not worthy to unloose" and comparatively John 1:27 in the Bible states, "He it is, who is coming after me is preferred before me, whose shoe's latchet I am not worthy to unloose." That is a curiously similar phrasing.

Continuing with the similarities, 1 Nephi 11:27 states, "And I looked and beheld the Redeemer of the world, of whom my father had spoken; and I also beheld the prophet who should prepare the way before him. And the Lamb of God went forth and was baptized of him; and after he was baptized, I beheld the heavens open, and the Holy Ghost come down out of heaven and abide upon him in the form of a dove."

This is undoubtedly similar to John 1:29-34 where there are phrases such as, "Behold the Lamb of God," and "therefore am I come baptizing with water," and "I saw the Spirit descending from heaven like a dove." What an uncanny resemblance.

In Romans 7:24 the Bible says, "O wretched man that I am!" Likewise, in 2 Nephi 4:17 it states, "O wretched man that I am!" The phrasing is identical. The second book of Nephi is basically restating the entire book of Isaiah, 2 Nephi 12:1 starting with, "The word that Isaiah, the son of Amoz, saw concerning Judah and Jerusalem."

In Hebrews 13:8, God says, "Jesus Christ the same yesterday, and today, and forever," this also parallels 1 Nephi 10:18, saying, "For he is the same yesterday, to-day, and forever." Yet another curiously similar verse. Noting all of the similarities in phraseology between the Book of Mormon and the King James Version of the Bible is important, as I believe it establishes a pattern of similarity that is unfounded. The thought process becomes, 'if the Bible says these things, and the Book of Mormon sounds just like the Bible, then they must both be true'. In fact, the Book of Mormon was made to appear and sound like the Bible for purposes of deception and establishing false ideals.

It is also important to note that there are several inconsistencies in the Mormon Doctrine. 1 Nephi 1:21 mentions the Lamb of God, which is actually a reference to New Testament language which was not seen until the book of John, after the coming of Christ. It is interesting the writers of the Book of Mormon would have been familiar with this language, prior to the coming of Jesus and the New Testament.

Along this same line of inconsistency, I would cite the Book of Mormon, Alma 46:15, "And those who did belong to the church were faithful; yea, all those who were true believers in Christ took upon them, gladly, the name of Christ, or Christians as they were called, because of their belief in Christ who should come." This part of the Book of Mormon was said by the Mormon's own records to be written around 73B.C.

I make note of this because this is the first time in the Book of Mormon that people were said to be called Christians. However, this directly contradicts the Bible in Acts 11:26, which says, "...For a whole year they met with the church and taught a great many people. And in Antioch the disciples were first called Christians." So – how can it be possible for the people in the book of Alma within the Book of Mormon to be called Christians when that term was to be coined many years later, according to the Bible?

Not Guilty by Reason of Human Error

In the Bible, 1 Corinthians 2:13, it says, "Which things also we speak, not in the words which man's wisdom teacheth, but which the Holy Ghost teacheth; comparing spiritual things with spiritual." The Bible is saying that the words of the Bible are not taught by human wisdom, but actually taught by God, through the Holy Spirit. Again this is reiterated in 2 Peter 1:20-21, saying "Knowing this first; that no prophecy of the scripture is of any private interpretation. For the prophecy came not in old time by the will of man..."

This is again clearly saying that prophecy does not come from someone's interpretation. It also clearly says that no prophecy was produced at the will of man. To me, this contradicts the act of praying to God and receiving 'revelations' that answer your questions.

You cannot prompt prophecy from God; it is just given to you. That being said, if 2 Peter says prophecy cannot be prompted, what can we make of the 'Question & Answer' session Joseph Smith had with God regarding the book of Revelations in the Bible?

To take that concept one step further, we only need to look into the Book of Mormon. The Book of Mormon readily admits that it is the word of man, and not the divine work of God. For example, in 1 Nephi 19:4-6, it says, "...these plates should be handed down from one generation to another, or from one prophet to another, until further commandments of the Lord. And an account of my making these plates shall be given hereafter; and then, behold, I proceed according to that which I have spoken; and this I do that the more sacred things may be kept for the knowledge of my people. Nevertheless, *I do not write anything upon plates save it be that I think it be sacred. And now, if I do err, even did they err of old; not that I would excuse myself because of other men, but because of the weakness which is in me, according to the flesh, I would excuse myself.*"

This section of in 1 Nephi openly suggests errors in the Book of Mormon due to the weakness of man. The Bible claims no such weakness, as its writings are a result of the words of the Holy Spirit, and not of man.

Again, in 1 Nephi 1:3, at the very beginning of the Book of Mormon it says, "And I know that the record which I make is true; and I make it with mine own hand; and I make it *according to my knowledge.*" If the Book of Mormon was a divine book, it would be made by the knowledge of God, and not the knowledge of a man as it claims of its own accord.

One thing that never truly made sense to me was the whole 'interpretation' factor. Mormons maintain that over time and due to translation and corruption by those in power, the Bible and its contents became increasingly erroneous. To that end, I would argue that in the LDS Church's own records, there have been over 1,000 corrections made to the book of the Mormon. Some were grammatical, some errors in transcription, some printing errors, etc.

But here is the real difference. There is no physical evidence of the golden plates on which Joseph Smith claimed the contents of the Book of Mormon were written. There are, however, hundreds of ancient transcripts of the Bible over thousands of years of history that still exist today and have been studied by modern-day scholars. Thousands of scholars have worked tirelessly to preserve the integrity of the Bible, not pervert it.

Tell Mormons to look at their own records. In 1830 they changed the text of 1 Nephi 11:18 from "Behold, the virgin which thou seest, is the Mother of God" to "Behold, the virgin which thou seest, is the Mother of the Son of God" in 1837. This hugely changes the meaning of the text, going from saying that Jesus is God to saying that he is not God.

So before Mormons begin casting stones at the Bible and its accuracy, perhaps they should look at their own doctrine first. Perhaps they would argue that Joseph Smith was just changing the text for comprehension. In that case, is changing the text for comprehension while not changing the meaning is okay for the Book of Mormon but not okay for the Bible?

That seems to be an unfair double standard, and this is a real point that Mormons have a difficult time arguing. Other than regurgitating the information they have been told that the "Bible was improperly translated and corrupted by those in power", they have little evidence to support those claims and little to say about the subject other than just that.

The words of the Book of Mormon further fall short of the truth in the Bible, if you look at the book of 2 Nephi. It is interesting to note in this chapter how the prophecies and visions of the 'Mormon prophets' were seemingly not divine.

First, if you look at 2 Nephi 11:1 it says, "And now, Jacob spake many more things to my people at that time; nevertheless, only these things have I caused to be written, for the things which I have written *sufficeth me*." In other words, the words he wrote were good enough for him, and he makes no mention of God.

Again in 2 Nephi 25:7, there is again reference to his own word, saying, "But behold, *I proceed with mine own prophecy,* according to *my plainness*; in which I know that no man can err."

I find it interesting that Nephi would refer to himself as a prophet, and speak to proceeding with his own prophecy, with again no mention of God or the Holy Spirit.

One last time in 2 Nephi 33:3, it is said, "But I, Nephi, having written what I have written, and *I esteem it as of great worth*, and especially unto my people." It is interesting to me that throughout the book of 2 Nephi, there is a tone of personal importance and self-worth, with again less importance being placed upon God and God's words.

As I mentioned in the chapter regarding the Mormon Word, the Book of Mormon is set out more as a history and an account of the people in America, and less a divine and inerrant book written by God. That being said, I would again reference the Book of Mormon and specifically the book of Jacob, 7:26 saying "...Wherefore, I conclude this record, declaring that I have written according *to the best of my knowledge.*"

On the whole, I do have several major hang-ups about the Book of Mormon and its 'divine' nature. The Bible readily states that the words of the Bible are not subject to the wisdom of man, but are the divine word of God through the Holy Spirit. Why then would God permit another scripture to be written which is openly subject to the errors and wisdom of man?

Furthermore, I would argue that God has provided us with the information that He knew was pertinent to our lives and salvation. Christ would not have left His work undone. In that same line of thought and referencing 2 Nephi 33:3 again, the Mormon doctrine shows that Nephi was providing what information *he* esteemed to be of great worth. As a result, I would say that the words in the Bible are God's words, and the words in the Book of Mormon are man's words.

Random Rules

While Mormons will argue that the Book of Mormon was from the same era as the Bible, they will admit that the Doctrine & Covenants and the Pearl of Great Price are not as they are books of revelation, not history. If that is the case, then why is it that there are chapters and chapters in the Doctrine & Covenants that add rules, ordinances and covenants to those that were addressed in the Bible? Even if there were some parts of the Bible translated incorrectly or missing, wouldn't it be a bit much to conclude that three entire scriptures worth of Bible was missing?

The reason why the 'Doctrine & Covenants' is named the Doctrine and Covenants is because it is just that. The term 'doctrine' means instructions or teachings, and 'covenants' means binding agreement. Mormons believe that they make binding agreements with God to obey the teachings and instructions in the Mormon scriptures.

The Mormon rulebook is unbelievably long, outlining regulations and restrictions that all Mormons must follow. There are many additional rules provided in the Mormon scriptures than there are provided in the Bible. I would argue again that these are additions and alterations to the original intent of the Bible, and I believe that it is important to pinpoint these alterations as some of them are very explanatory of the Mormon way of life.

In Mormonism, as in most Christianity, the Mormon Church strongly believes that it is their life goal to bring people to their faith. People are instructed to give up their own property for the sake of the church, "And again, I command thee that thou shalt not covet thine own property, but impart it freely to the printing of the Book of Mormon, which contains the truth and the word of God" Doctrine & Covenants 19:26.

To them, it is God's instruction to print the Book of Mormon and provide it to everyone possible. Ever wonder why the hotel desk drawer often has a Book of Mormon shoved in it?

The Mormon Church also speaks to the topic of forgiveness. In mainstream Christianity, there is a strong and sincere belief in forgiveness. It is difficult for many people to understand this type of unconditional forgiveness. I would relate our forgiveness of others to God's unconditional forgiveness of us through grace.

However, Mormon doctrine teaches that there are stipulations on forgiveness in the cases of murder and adultery. "And now, behold, I speak unto the church. Thou shalt not kill; and he that kills shall not have forgiveness in this world, nor in the world to come. And again, I say, thou shalt not kill; but he that killeth shall die" Doctrine & Covenants 42:18-19. Whereas in mainstream Christianity we believe in grace, Mormons believe is grace plus works, minus the unforgivable acts. Interesting rule. Not in the Bible.

Another unforgiveable act is adultery, but the stipulations for adultery are different. "Thou shalt not commit adultery; and he that committeth adultery, and repenteth not, shall be cast out. But he that has committed adultery and repents with all his heart, and forsaketh it, and doeth it no more, thou shalt forgive; But if he doeth it again, he shall not be forgiven, but shall be cast out" Doctrine & Covenants 42:24-26. So, you have a get-out-of-jail-free card. If you commit adultery once and repent, you are forgiven. But if you do it again, you cannot be forgiven. Interesting rule. Not in the Bible.

Adultery is not limited to an actual act either. It can actually come from impure thoughts and feelings, as well. "And verily I say unto you, as I have said before, he that looketh on a woman to lust after her, or if any shall commit adultery in their hearts, they shall not have the Spirit, but shall deny the faith and shall fear. Wherefore, I, the Lord, have said that the fearful, and the unbelieving, and all liars, and whosoever loveth and maketh a lie, and the whoremonger, and the sorcerer, shall have their part in that lake which burneth with fire and brimstone, which is the second death. Verily, I say that they shall not have part in the first resurrection" Doctrine & Covenants 63:16-18.

There is such great fear in the Mormon community of ever doing any wrong, even in their own hearts. Many would say that they live a 'sheltered' existence in their own communities, out of fear of exposure to things that are common in mainstream society.

Experiencing any impure feelings or thoughts is synonymous with denial of their faith and sacrificing the first resurrection – spending a thousand years in hell. Interesting rule. Not in the Bible.

Another interesting twist on forgiveness and sin is written into Doctrine & Covenants 132:26-27, "…if a man marry a wife according to my word, and they are sealed by the Holy Spirit of promise, according to mine appointment, and he or she shall commit any sin or transgression of the new and everlasting covenant whatever, and all manner of blasphemies, and if they commit no murder wherein they shed innocent blood, yet they shall come forth in the first resurrection, and enter into their exaltation; but they shall be destroyed in the flesh, and shall be delivered unto the buffetings of Satan unto the day of redemption…" Doctrine & Covenants 132:26.

This passage is a bit confusing but generally says that those who are married in the temple but do not keep their temple covenants with God will be resurrected, but then found guilty of their sins and then sent to hell. Again, this is a complete disregard for the concept of grace and further illustrates the rituals within Mormonism for salvation. Interesting rule. Not in the Bible.

And again, "Wherefore, I say unto you, that ye ought to forgive one another; for he that forgiveth not his brother his trespasses standeth condemned before the Lord; for there remaineth in him the greater sin. I, the Lord, will forgive whom I will forgive, but of you it is required to forgive all men. And ye ought to say in your hearts – let God judge between me and thee, and reward thee according to thy deeds" Doctrine & Covenants 64:9-10.

First, it is interesting that there are exceptions to this forgiveness such as murder, but here the text contradicts itself by saying that all people must forgive. So I suppose that you must forgive unless one of the previous conditions for not forgiving is met? Or perhaps only God can choose not to forgive, so thereby He is not truly an example to us? There is also a tone in this verse of competition for 'Godliness' amongst Mormons, saying that since each is rewarded according to their deeds they stand in constant judgment of each other. In my opinion, it is standing in that judgment by fellow members of the church that is the greatest turn-off for many caught in the life of Mormonism.

Of course, despite the rules provided for murders, adulterers and forgiveness, there are still more rules for how to interact with others. The

Doctrine and Covenants chapter 98 goes back and forth on this issue, saying that if your enemy attacks you and repents and asks your forgiveness, you should forgive him.

If he does it the first time and does not repent, you should forgive him regardless, and forgive him again the second and third times. "But if he trespass against thee the fourth time thou shalt not forgive him, but shalt bring these testimonies before the Lord; and they shall not be blotted out until he repent and reward thee four-fold in all things wherewith he has trespassed against thee. And if he do this, thou shalt forgive him with all thine heart; and if he do not this, I, the Lord, will avenge thee of thine enemy a hundred-fold" Doctrine & Covenants 98:44-45.

So as confusing as this may be, if he attacks you a fourth time, you should not forgive him and the Lord will avenge those wrong-doings by rewarding you and not forgive him until he repents. Now not only is our God a good God, but he has also become a vindictive God.

To add to the vengeance, he will not only avenge your enemies but also your enemies' children, "…upon his children, and upon his children's children of all them that hate me, unto the third and fourth generation. But if the children shall repent, or the children's children, and turn to the Lord their God, with all their hearts and with all their might, mind and strength, they restore four-fold all their trespasses wherewith they have trespassed, or wherewith their fathers have trespassed, or their father's fathers, then thine indignation shall be turned away; and vengeance shall no more come upon them, saith the Lord thy God, and their trespasses shall never be brought any more as a testimony before the Lord against them. Amen" Doctrine & Covenants 98:46-48.

These particular verses really had me thinking once I read them, because it is apparent to me that these verses contradict the Book of Mormon itself. In the second Mormon article of faith, they say that they believe that men will be punished for their own sins and not for Adam's transgressions.

It is fundamental to Mormonism that they don't believe in original sin and they believe that all members have the autonomy and can 'choose the right'. If you believe that men will be punished for their own sins, then why in this particular case are the children to be punished for the sins of their ancestors? Why should the child have to repent for the sins of the parent?

To me this doctrine contradicts itself, because you cannot declare your autonomy in the same breath that you ask for forgiveness for a past full of sins that were not yours.

Just as works are important in the LDS faith, behavior is as well. In fact, Mormons believe that they are commanded to not only behave well at all times, but also to watch each other and instruct each other on how to behave.

"And now, behold, I give unto you a commandment, that when ye are assembled together ye shall instruct and edify each other, that ye may know how to act and direct my church, how to act upon the points of my law and commandments, which I have given. And thus ye shall become instructed in the law of my church, and be sanctified by that which ye have received, and ye shall bind yourselves to act in all holiness before me – That inasmuch as ye do this, glory shall be added to the kingdom which ye have received Inasmuch as ye do it not, it shall be taken, even that which ye have received" Doctrine & Covenants 43:8-10.

Throughout the history of Christianity, there have been traditional days that are reserved for abstinence from specific things. One such example is abstaining from meat on Ash Wednesday and every Friday during the duration of Lent.

Interestingly enough, the Mormon doctrine addresses these sacrifices as well, saying "And whoso forbiddeth to abstain from meats, that man should not eat the same, is not ordained of God; for behold, the beasts of the field and the fowls of the air, and that which cometh of the earth, is ordained for the use of man for food and for raiment, and that he might have abundance" Doctrine & Covenants 49:18-19.

This verse is directly contradicting fundamental Christian traditions, saying not only that it is unnecessary to abstain from meat, but that whoever started the tradition was not of God. This directly attacks both mainstream Christianity and the traditions that have been alive within Christianity since its establishment. However, while Mormons oppose cutting out meat on specific days, they are not opposed to fasting altogether. I remember my parents fasting on the first Sunday of every month, which was particularly difficult when church was three hours long.

"But remember that on this, the Lord's day, thou shalt offer thine oblations and thy sacraments unto the Most High, confessing thy sins unto thy brethren, and before the Lord. And on this day thou shalt do none other thing, only let thy food be prepared with a singleness of heart that thy fasting may be perfect, or, in other words, that thy joy may be full. Verily, this is fasting and prayer, or in other words, rejoicing and prayer" Doctrine & Covenants 59:12-14.

I would argue that Mormons fast under the same principles that mainstream Christians may decline to eat meat on particular holidays. It seems a bit silly to recognize the importance of one yet decline the significance of another.

One of my most vivid memories from my childhood is bearing of testimonies. The first Sunday of every month is for the bearing of testimonies. Now that I am older, I realize that Pastors spend a great deal of time coming up with solid lessons for their congregations each Sunday.

Regardless of the contemporary or conservative settings of each church, the message remains solid and is the center of your church day. One solid hour of good, Biblically based, life lessons. On the first Sunday of the month in the LDS church, it is one solid hour of people walking up to the pulpit and bearing their testimonies.

Sometimes it was a three year old, being held up to the microphone by his mother, her whispering in his ear what to say and him repeating it to the congregation. Sometimes it was an elderly person, sometimes a family friend, and sometimes the bishop. "Nevertheless, ye are blessed, for the testimony which ye have borne is recorded in heaven for the angels to look upon; and they rejoice over you, and your sins are forgiven you" Doctrine & Covenants 62:3.

One solid hour of people walking up to the microphone with the first sentence out of each of their mouths being 'I'd like to bear my testimony that I know this church is true, and Joseph Smith was the true prophet'. While most mainstream Christian churches encourage the profession of faith, Mormons mandate it as yet another work.

The New & Everlasting Covenant…and Eternity

Mormons call the new rules and ordinances the 'New and Everlasting Covenant'. This covenant is actually a compilation of all of the covenants that the Mormon doctrine confers upon its people.

To Mormons, not following this everlasting covenant is a denial of your salvation entirely, as said in Doctrine & Covenants 132:6, "And as pertaining to the new and everlasting covenant, it was instituted for the fullness of my glory; and he that receiveth a fullness thereof must and shall abide by the law, or he shall be damned, saith the Lord God."

Beyond this, Mormons believe that there are conditions to the laws of God, the first being again that those things which are sealed on earth are sealed in heaven. Mormons believe that spouses or families not sealed in the Mormon temple will never see each other again in heaven.

They also believe as Joseph claimed of himself, that there can only be one prophet on the earth at a time. This is shown in Doctrine & Covenants 132:7, "And verily I say unto you, that the conditions of this law are these: All covenants, contracts, bonds, obligations, oaths, vows, performances, connections, association, or expectations, that are not made and entered into and sealed by the Holy Spirit of promise, of him who is anointed, both as well for time and for all eternity, and that too most holy, by revelation and commandment through the medium of mine anointed, whom I have appointed on the earth to hold this power (and I have appointed unto my servant Joseph to hold this power in the last days, and there is never but one on the earth at a time on whom this power and the keys of this priesthood are conferred), are of no efficacy, virtue, or force I and after the resurrection from the dead; for all contracts that are not made unto this end have an end when men are dead."

Clearly expressed, because mainstream Christians do not share the Mormon belief and are not sealed to each other on earth, we will not share in their ability to see our loved ones again after our death. From my perspective, the mandate of temple sealing is a function only of the Mormon Doctrine, and not of the Bible.

This is another example of how the Mormon doctrines will fill-in-the-blanks of the Bible. The Bible may be unclear regarding what happens in heaven, but it is my belief that God gave us just as much information as he intended and that the Mormon methodology of sealing families together is yet another example of adding to the intent of the Bible, and filling in what the Bible leaves out.

Throughout the Book of Mormon and the Doctrine & Covenants, there are many restatements, revised explanations and contradictions. Many mainstream Christians will argue that opening yourself to understanding the Mormon doctrine is dangerous ground. I would sincerely disagree. Mormons are fundamentally and doctrinally different than mainstream Christians.

Belief in additional scriptures and revelations are part of worship in the Mormon Church, and it is so important to understand what those beliefs are and where the errors and changes in their doctrine reside before you can witness to a person of the Mormon faith. Being able to identify where these changes, revisions, restatements and errors lie may open doors to Christianity that were previously closed in that person's life.

Law & Church

Ironically, while Mormons maintain that no one can gain salvation except themselves, they also claim in the tenth article of faith: We claim the privilege of worshiping the Almighty God according to the dictates of our own conscience, and allow all men the same privilege, let them worship how, where, or what they may. So, everyone else can worship God as they wish, but only Mormons are right.

They also state in the eleventh article of faith: We believe in being subject to kings, presidents, rulers, and magistrates, in obeying, honoring and sustaining the law. While Mormons believe in upholding man's law, they are very strongly tied to their faith and the ultimate law – God's law.

God Wrote the Constitution

It is interesting to note the similarities between the laws provided to Joseph Smith by God in Doctrine & Covenants chapter 98, and the laws of man at the time Joseph Smith was establishing the church. I would contend that most mainstream Christian churches also believe strongly in following the laws of man, so long as they do not contradict those laws given by God through his Word.

However, Mormons take this a step further, incorporating those words of man-made law into their doctrine, and therefore into their 'divine' texts. "And now, verily I say unto you concerning the laws of the land, it is my will that my people should observe to do all things whatsoever I command them. And that law of the land which is constitutional, supporting that principle of freedom in maintaining rights and privileges, belongs to all mankind, and is justifiable before me. Therefore, I, the Lord, justify you, and your brethren of my church, in befriending the law which is the constitutional law of the land; and as pertaining to the law of man, whatsoever is more of less than this, cometh of evil. I, the Lord God, make you free, therefore ye are free indeed; and the law also maketh you free" Doctrine & Covenants 98:4-8.

There are several key words in these verses which would suggest that this revelation is specific to a framework of time, and therefore influenced by man and not entirely the words of God. Those words are 'constitutional' and 'freedom'.

This revelation was said to occur in August of 1833, when the United States constitution was still in its infancy and slavery was prevalent. I would suggest that these revelations were a result of the influence of Joseph Smith's physical surroundings, rather than the direct revelations of God.

Mormons are firm in their belief to follow all leaders, as they state in their eleventh article of faith. This is primarily because they believe that God is the influence of all governments, and not promoting governmental laws and sanctions would therefore be turning your back on God. This is stated in Doctrine & Covenants 134:1, "We believe that governments were instituted of God for the benefit of man; and that he holds men accountable for their acts in relation to them, both in making laws and administering them, for the good and safety of society."

These beliefs were declared during a church assembly in 1835, when compiling the content of what would be the first edition of the Doctrine & Covenants. I would argue that instead of just saying to abide by the man-made law, the Doctrine & Covenants actually establishes a set of laws which are similar to those provided in the U.S. Constitution.

They continue, "We believe that no government can exist in peace, except such laws are framed and held inviolate as will secure to each individual the free exercise of conscience, the right and control of property, and the protection of life. We believe that all governments necessarily require civil officers and magistrates to enforce the laws of the same; and that such as will administer the law in equity and justice should be sought for and upheld by the voice of the people if a republic, or the will of the sovereign" Doctrine & Covenants 134:2-3.

It is interesting in this particular portion of the Mormon doctrine that they actually appear to be establishing the law of the land as is to be applicable to the Mormon people. If you have ever visited or lived in Utah (I was born there), it is very apparent that there are both spiritual and civil laws that all people abide by. To me, this makes Utah seem like a little Utopia in America; a society created inside of a man-made bubble.

"We believe that religion is instituted of God; and that men are amenable to him, and to him only, for the exercise of it, unless their religious opinions prompt them to infringe upon the rights and liberties of others; but we do not believe that human law has a right to interfere with prescribing rules of worship to bind the consciences of men, nor dictate forms for public or private devotion; that the civil magistrate should restrain crime, but never control conscience; should punish guilt, but never suppress the freedom of the soul" Doctrine & Covenants 134:4.

This verse is a lengthy restatement of the first amendment of the United States, stating the freedom of religion for all Americans. Again, this was largely influenced by the period of the establishment of the church, when the Constitution was in its infancy.

This was elaborated upon in Doctrine & Covenants 134:5, "We believe that all men are bound to sustain and uphold the respective governments in which they reside, while protected in their inherent and inalienable rights by the laws of such governments; and that sedition and rebellion are unbecoming every citizen thus protected, and should be punished accordingly; and that all governments have a right to enact such laws as in their own judgments are best calculated to secure the public interest; at the same time, however, holding sacred the freedom of conscience."

This particular verse is calling out to the Mormon people again to be bound and abide by the laws of man. At the same time, however, this verse is condemning sedition and rebellion by the people, and somewhat demanding their compliance. All people should fall in line with the laws of man and God, or be punished.

Handling the Bad Apples

The Mormon lifestyle is very much about control. The Mormon Church and its people exercise control and are commanded to watch over each other, ensuring that all the people of the church are doing exactly as they are told. "We believe that every man should be honored in his station, rulers and magistrates as such, being placed for the protection of the innocent and the punishment of the guilty; and that to the laws all men show respect and deference, as without them peace and harmony would be supplanted by anarchy and terror; human laws being instituted for the express purpose of regulating our interests as individuals and nations, between man and man; and divine laws given of heaven, prescribing rules on spiritual concerns, for faith and worship, both to be answered by man to his Maker" Doctrine & Covenants 134:6.

The laws of God and the laws of man are not independent of each other in Mormonism. Since the laws and governments of man were established by God, Mormons must follow both to gain their salvation.

As we have established, Mormons interrelate the laws of man and the laws of God. In this light, they also reserve the right to punish or excommunicate those members of their faith for breaking the laws of man and God. "We believe that all religious societies have a right to deal with their members for disorderly conduct, according to the rules and regulations of such societies; provided that such dealings be for fellowship and good standing; but we do not believe that any religious society has the authority to try men on the right of property or life, to take from them this world's goods, or to put them in jeopardy of either life or limb, or to inflict any physical punishment upon them. They can only excommunicate them from their society, and withdraw from them their fellowship" Doctrine & Covenants 134:10.

Within Mormonism, the absolute worst punishment that can be installed would be excommunication. For example, while murder is a criminal offense which will be prosecuted by the laws of man, the ultimate punishment the church can impose would be spiritual exile through excommunication.

Another prime example of the influence of these laws dictated by the timing of the establishment of the Mormon Church is Doctrine & Covenants 134:12, "We believe it just to preach the gospel to the nation of the earth, and warn the righteous to save themselves from the corruption of the world; but we do not believe it right to interfere with bond-servants, neither preach the gospel to, not baptize them contrary to the will and wish of their masters, nor to meddle with or influence them in the least to cause them to be dissatisfied with their situations in this life, thereby jeopardizing the lives of men; such interference we believe to be unlawful and unjust, and dangerous to the peace of every government allowing human beings to be held in servitude." Mormons generally did not believe in slavery and discouraged slave holding amongst its members.

However, I find one thing about this statement interesting. It is the ultimate goal of all Christians to preach the Word to all people, despite circumstances and fear. There are many stories in the Bible and throughout history when people placed themselves in harm's way, in an effort to bring people to God and teach them about Jesus. There are also stories of great trials and tribulations, when men suffered greatly under the careful watch of God.

Why then, under the circumstances of servitude, would God request that people not put themselves in the way of harm to preach His word? If we will all be accountable for accepting Jesus in our lives on Judgment Day, why would Mormons permit servants to be damned to hell simply to save their own physical lives? In my opinion, that is self-serving and not Christ-like at all.

Mormon Missionaries

I am sure you have seen them. Young men around nineteen years of age; riding on bikes dressed in their Sunday suits and wearing a backpack and a helmet. Mormon missionaries. Perhaps one has come to your door, spoken with you or asked you whether or not you've read the Book of Mormon.

Growing up, the missionaries were a common occurrence in our house. Every Sunday it was our job as church-goers to make sure that the missionaries had dinner. I loved when the missionaries would come over because my mother would make the good stuff – the really great meals that taste even better when you eat them off of mom's fine china.

The Mormon Church is a proselytizing church, meaning they send missionaries all over the world to spread the Mormon gospel. It is a constant topic of discussion in the Mormon Church, as spreading their faith is one of the most important facets to their Christianity.

It could be said that the LDS church has one of the most active missionary programs in existence today. They are incredibly diligent and organized in this activity, as you can image from their structure of their church hierarchy. There are currently more than 55,000 full-time missionaries serving around the world, and they perform these services unpaid. Male missionaries are more common, and are called Elders. Female missionaries are far less common, but are called Sisters and do serve similarly to their male counterparts – as much as they can without holding the priesthood.

Missionaries will preach in any corner of the world that will permit them to be there. A typical mission lasts for two years for men, starting at the age of 19. Women are allowed to go on a mission for a year and a half, starting the age of 21. My father, grandfather, uncles, and nearly all of the men in my family – both sides – have served on a Mormon mission.

In fact, that is why my Father, Uncle and Grandfather can now speak fluent Spanish. They all served full time missions in foreign, Spanish-speaking countries. There are two types of missionaries – full time and part time. Full time missionaries will teach in places far from their home, all over the world. Part time missions, sometimes called stake missions, will perform this same work in their local communities.

The mission work of the church took off in 1974, when the Mormon prophet Spencer Kimball had a revelation, and subsequently called out to the young men of the church asking them to go on missions. The church, however, had been a missionary church for some time before that. Joseph Smith's brother, Samuel Smith, was the first missionary. It was actually Samuel Smith who converted Brigham Young, who turned out to be the second prophet of the Mormon Church.

Why the extensive mission work? Not unlike many churches, mission work helps the church to grow and spreads their gospel. They point to Jeremiah 16:16, saying "Behold, I will send for many fishers, saith the LORD, and they shall fish them; and after will I send for many hunters, and they shall hunt them from every mountain, and from every hill, and out of the holes of the rocks." This concept of mission work is not foreign or lost in mainstream Christianity, and in fact many people do serve missions, go on mission trips, and help people in their communities.

Mission work for all Christian faiths is certainly encouraged. Within the Mormon Church, it is an expectation and a requirement. A young man and his family are expected to pay their own way, or request that the ward help them finance their mission. Just like college, many Mormon families will save money to send their sons on missions prior to college.

If they cannot afford to pay for the mission themselves, the Mormon doctrine calls upon the people of the church to support their mission efforts, "Behold, I say unto you, that it is the duty of the church to assist in supporting the families of those, and also to support the families of those who are called and must needs be sent unto the world to proclaim the gospel unto the world" Doctrine & Covenants 75:24.

There are requirements for young men and women to be permitted to go on a mission. They must be active members in the Mormon Church, they must be worthy to enter the temple, they must have obeyed the Word of Wisdom and they must have moral cleanliness. Mormon men must also have the Melchizedek priesthood, which is the power of God that Mormons believe allows them to act in the name of God to conduct baptisms and other necessary ordinances in the LDS church.

Once they submit their name to the church, the Quorum of the Twelve Apostles will review their application. Through divine revelation, they will determine where that specific missionary should go. They will assign each missionary on a specific mission, in one of their approximately 330 mission destinations. Being 'called' on a mission is a very prideful thing for the young man's family.

There are approximately seventeen Missionary Training Centers to which the selected individual may report, dependent upon their location around the globe. At this training center, they will receive extensive language training so they can speak the language of the country in which they will reside. They will also study the Mormon scriptures and learn how to teach them to others, as well as learn and prepare themselves for life as a missionary.

If the missionary already speaks the language of the location they have been assigned, they may only stay at the missionary training center for about three weeks. If they must learn a foreign language, they may be at the missionary training center for up to ten weeks. If for any reason a missionary training center is unavailable to the potential missionary, a local church can be used as a training center instead. After several weeks of preparation and training, missionaries will depart for their assigned mission, which they fondly refer to as 'entering the mission field'.

Again, with structure. Every mission area is divided into zones and districts, and will have several missionaries working underneath it. Each zone and district will be led by a Mission President. The Mission President will supervise the missionaries, review weekly statistics and assign them different territories within their mission field.

When a person is 'called' to be a Mission President, they typically will move their family to the mission location to serve a three-year term. Not unlike the classic church hierarchy, two Mormon Missionaries will be called to be Assistants to the President and will help him with organizing and administering policies to the missionaries beneath him.

The missionaries will always work in pairs. They will work together and share the same living space. This is probably partially for safety, but the Mormons site Mark 6:7, "And he called [unto him] the twelve, and began to send them forth by two and two; and gave them power over unclean spirits." These partnerships will typically last several months before they are switched to a different area.

You may have noticed that Mormon missionaries are all very similar in appearance. Missionaries are required to wear white shirts with ties, dark suits, and have their hair cut short. Women must wear dresses or skirts. All missionaries must also wear name tags, showing that they are members of the LDS church.

They are not allowed to have inappropriate contact with members of the opposite sex. They must stay with their companion at all times, and there is absolutely no media communication allowed unless it is authorized by the Mormon Church.

Not unlike many mission trips served by Christian churches around the globe, missionaries typically spend much of their time in service. It is mandated that while in the mission field, they perform a minimum of 10 hours of community service per week. They believe that in doing so, they are following in Christ's example of service.

Being away from your family for two years is very difficult. Missionaries are not allowed to come home for the duration of their two year mission trip. Returned Missionaries (often called RM's in Mormon circles) are highly revered by their home churches for their service to the church. Many consider it a sacrifice to be away for so long, but for most they consider it an honor.

Young men of the Mormon Church are not the only people allowed to pursue the missionary experience. Many senior members of the church will elect to undergo a second mission trip, or go on a first trip if they never had the chance to go in their youth.

These Senior Missionaries are often companioned by their spouse or with a fellow partner as the younger missionaries are. Senior Missionaries will undergo a very similar process to their younger counterparts, also attending the Missionary Training Center before their mission departure. However, the Senior Missionaries will often be working in a more specific capacity, serving in the fields of genealogy or humanitarianism.

Those missionaries whose primary purpose is to teach the Mormon Gospel are proselytizing missionaries. The LDS Church also has what they call Church Service Missionaries, or missionaries who perform non-gospel driven missions. These Church Service Missionaries may serve full-time missions, but will be primarily performing community service, leadership training, technical missions and humanitarian training.

The LDS Church has a program called the LDS Foundation, which oversees all of the humanitarian efforts of the church. Many of the Church Service Missionaries will work for those church-led organizations to promote their efforts. This is often a position that is a calling for many of the elderly couples in the church.

The Mormon Church is extremely effective in their missionary work, having the structure and manpower to spread their beliefs rapidly. For this reason, they have been growing exponentially in size over the past several decades. They propagate false ideals about God and His plan for us, and it is unbelievably important that we not only understand what they are saying, but also understand how to explain to others why these teachings are untrue.

Marriage & Polygamy

I hate this topic. The subject of polygamy brings up bad childhood memories when people would ask me how many moms I had, or if I had a hundred siblings. To answer the question – nope, just me, my mom, my dad, one brother and one sister. One mom, two siblings, no crazy family with 27 kids.

Polygamy is one of the most hotly debated topics in the Mormon Church's history. Up until the revelation provided to Wilford Woodruff in 1890, Mormons believed in polygamy. Polygamy is the practice of plural marriage, or having more than one spouse. While it is difficult for most men to imagine having more than just one wife (yes, the nagging would be multiplied), this was an active practice in the Mormon Church for many years.

Polygamy makes a Comeback

Why exactly did Mormons believe that polygamy needed to exist? Mormons say that the answer to this question is only known by God. However, many have speculated that polygamy was instated for several reasons. First, polygamy was a way in which the number of Mormon members of the church could be rapidly increased.

Second, there were many more women in the Mormon faith than men at this time, primarily due to war. Some members felt that this was a way for all of the women of the church to be cared after under those circumstances, as well as a means by which to drastically grow the church population.

The act of polygamy in the Mormon Church was actually started as part of an inquiry from Joseph Smith to God. Joseph asked God about the practice of polygamy in the Old Testament, referring to Abraham (who married Sarah and Hagar), Jacob (the father of the twelve tribes of Israel and married sisters Leah and Rachel), King Saul and King David. Mormons believe that through divine revelation, God told Joseph Smith that the act of polygamy should be reinstated as a religious principle. For the purposes of explaining their reasoning behind this, I will cite extensively the Doctrine & Covenants, chapter 132.

"Abraham received promises concerning his seed, and of the fruit of his loins – from whose loins ye are, namely, my servant Joseph – which were to continue so long as they were in the world; and as touching Abraham and his seed, out of the world they should continue; both in the world and out of the world they should continue as innumerable as the stars; or, if ye were to count the sand upon the seashore ye could not number them. This promise is *yours also*, because ye are of Abraham and the promise was made unto Abraham; and by this law is the continuation of the works of my Father, wherein he glorifieth himself. Go ye, therefore, and do the works of Abraham; enter ye into my law and ye shall be saved. But if ye enter not into my law ye cannot receive the promise of my Father, which he had made unto Abraham" Doctrine & Covenants 132:30-33.

Mormons are clearly citing the Old Testament practice, whereby the ultimate goal was procreation and therefore growth of the population. It was the original belief of the LDS Church that polygamy should be practiced to create more followers of the Mormon faith.

As Joseph appointed himself a descendant of Abraham, he was also entitled to the promises given to Abraham for practicing polygamy.

This thought is continued, saying, "God commanded Abraham, and Sarah gave Hagar to Abraham to wife. And why did she do it? Because this was the law; and from Hagar sprang many people. This, therefore, was fulfilling, among other things, the promises. Was Abraham, therefore, under condemnation? Verily I say unto you, Nay; for I, the Lord, commanded it. Abraham was commanded to offer his son Isaac; nevertheless, it was written: Thou shalt not kill. Abraham, however, did not refuse, and it was accounted unto him for righteousness. Abraham received concubines, and they bore him children; and it was accounted unto him for righteousness, because they were given unto him, and he abode in my law; as Isaac also and Jacob did none other things than that which they were commanded; and because they did none other things than that which they were commanded, they have entered into their exaltation, according to the promises, and sit upon the thrones, and *are not angels but are gods*" Doctrine & Covenants 132:34-37.

Joseph Smith, through his 'revelations' documented in the Doctrine & Covenants, is justifying polygamy in the present day as a commandment from God for the propagation of the Mormon beliefs.

Many wives could have many children, and therefore the Mormon Church could grow in size organically. Beyond the simple idea of growing the church through procreation, Joseph Smith creates the idea that polygamy is actually endorsed by God saying that Isaac, Jacob and Abraham are said not to be angels, but to actually be Gods for doing as God commanded by practicing polygamy.

"David also received many wives and concubines, and also Solomon and Moses my servants, as also many others of my servants, from the beginning of creation until this time; and in nothing did they sin save in those things which they received not of me. David's wives and concubines were given unto him of me, by the hand of Nathan, my servant, and others of the prophets who had the keys of this power; and in none of these things did he sin against me save in the case of Uriah and his wife; and, therefore he hath fallen from his exaltation, and received his portion; and he shall not inherit them out of the world, for I have them unto another, saith the Lord. I am the Lord thy God, and I gave unto thee, my servant Joseph, an appointment, and restore all things. Ask what ye will, and it shall be given unto you according to my word" Doctrine & Covenants 132:38-40.

These verses address David and his plural marriages, but explain his fall from exaltation – or failure to become a God – as a result of his relationship with Uriah's wife. It is then promised to Joseph Smith that he can have all things, if he would just ask for them.

One point of contention that I would make with the Doctrine & Covenants establishment of the acceptability of plural marriage is that it contradicts the Book of Mormon. If Mormons are to believe all of their doctrine, then how can they possibly believe two doctrines which contradict one another?

In the Book of Mormon, Jacob 2:23-24, it says, "But the word of God burdens me because of your grosser crimes. For behold, thus saith the Lord: this people begin to wax in iniquity; they understand not the scriptures, for they seek to excuse themselves in committing whoredoms, because of the things which were written concerning David, and Solomon his son. Behold, *David and Solomon truly had many wives and concubines, which thing was abominable before me*, saith the Lord."

If the Mormon's own Book of Mormon states that polygamy is abominable, then how can it be revealed to them that David is an example of polygamy as an acceptable practice?

The Nature of Marriage

The Bible is very specific about the nature of marriage from the very beginning. In Matthew 19:4-6, "And he answered and said unto them, have ye not read, that he which made them at the beginning made them male and female, and said, for this cause shall a man leave father and mother, and shall cleave to his wife: and they twain shall be one flesh? Wherefore they are no more twain, but one flesh. What therefore God hath joined together, let no man put asunder." Again, there is a mention of a man and a woman, singularly.

Joseph Smith, however, argued that the Bible promotes plural marriage. I believe that this plurality is taken out of context. In fact, the Bible warns against this behavior by explaining the evil effects of polygamous behavior.

This is shown in 1 Kings 11:1-11, "Now King Solomon loved many foreign women, along with the daughter of Pharaoh…You shall not enter into marriage with them, neither shall they with you, for surely they will turn away your heart after their gods. Solomon clung to these in love. He had 700 wives, princesses, and 300 concubines. And his wives turned away his heart. For when Solomon was old his wives turned away his heart after other gods, and his heart was not wholly true to the Lord his God, as was the heart of David his father…So Solomon did what was evil in the sight of the Lord and did not wholly follow the Lord, as David his father had done…Therefore the Lord said to Solomon, Since this has been your practice and you have not kept my covenant and my statues that I have commanded you, I will surely tear the kingdom from you and will give it to your servant."

So does practicing polygamy would fall under the category of adultery? Even at the time the Mormon Church was practicing polygamy, the answer to this question from the voice of mainstream Christianity was undoubtedly 'yes'. After all, adultery is a simple concept – being physically or emotionally intimate with a person outside of your marriage.

Polygamy encouraged that behavior. But what happens when the Mormon Church brings *multiple people* into a marriage *together*? Joseph answered this question through revelations, providing a series of circumstances under which certain actions were and were not considered to be adultery, and the severity of the punishment for those actions.

"And as ye have asked concerning adultery, verily, verily, I say unto you, if a man receiveth a wife in the new and everlasting covenant, and if she be with another man, and I have not appointed unto her by the holy anointing, she hath committed adultery and shall be destroyed. If she be not in the new and everlasting covenant, and she be with another man, she has committed adultery. And if her husband be with another woman, and he was under a vow, he hath broken his vow and hath committed adultery. And if she hath not committed adultery, but is innocent and hath not broken her vow, and she knoweth it, and I reveal it unto you, my servant Joseph, then you shall have the power, by the power of my Holy Priesthood, to take her and give her unto him that hath not committed adultery but hath been faithful; for he shall be made *ruler over many*" Doctrine & Covenants 41-44.

Long story short, if a woman is married in the temple and cheats on their spouse, she will be destroyed. However, if the infidelity is simply an accusation found by Joseph Smith to be untrue, Joseph Smith has the power to reinstate their marriage. Furthermore, the male of that unbroken relationship will be made ruler over many things, once again inferring exaltation and Godliness of man through their Mormon salvation.

The Mormon practice of polygamy has been sensationalized over time, and it should also be noted that less than a quarter of Mormons during that time ever even practiced the act. The only permissible way to be involved in a polygamous relationship within the Mormon Church was when it was called for by God through the acting Prophet of the church. The Mormon reputation of polygamy precedes itself, as a much smaller percentage of Mormons actually practiced polygamy than many would believe.

Don't Worry about it, God said it's Cool

The Mormon belief in polygamy was not simply a practice of people in the area. In fact, this belief is doctrinally sound within the Mormon faith and specified in the Doctrine & Covenants.

"And again, as pertaining to the law of the priesthood – if any man espouse a virgin and desire to espouse another, and the first give her consent, and if he espouse the second and they are virgins, and have vowed to no other man, then is he justified; he cannot commit adultery for they are given unto him; for he cannot commit adultery with that that belongeth unto him and no one else. And if he have ten virgins given unto him by this law, he cannot commit adultery, for they belong to him, and they are given unto him; therefore is he justified." Doctrine & Covenants 132:61-62. This verse is quite profound to me, as I believe it carries with it many meanings.

First, it is saying that within the priesthood carries the power of men to take upon themselves many wives as long as they are all virgins. Second, I believe that it speaks a great deal to the way women are viewed within the Mormon Church. As a young women in the church, I felt that it was my only duty to get married young and have children, and that my importance as a person was little more than that.

Yes, yes, Mormons will argue that this is untrue and unfair, but it's a personal opinion. Look at Utah, look at how young people get married, and look at their roles in society. It is my opinion that this verse further supports those feelings, demonstrating that wives are possessions 'given unto them' and that polygamy is not adultery because you cannot cheat on someone that 'belongeth unto him and no one else'.

Women were not viewed as spiritual partners, to which a man was to devote his life honoring and protecting. They were little more than property, belonging to a man for the purpose of growing the church.

This doctrine is further explained, "But if one or either of the ten virgins, after she is espoused, shall be with another man, she has committed adultery, and shall be destroyed; for they are given unto him to multiply and replenish the earth, according to my commandment, and to fulfill the promise which was given by my Father before the foundation of the world, and for their exaltation in the eternal worlds, that they may bear the souls of men; for herein is the work of my Father continued, that he may be glorified. And again, verily, verily, I say unto you, if any man have a wife, who holds the keys of this power, and he teaches unto her the law of my priesthood, as pertaining to these things, then she shall believe and administer unto him, or she shall be destroyed, saith the Lord your God; for I will destroy her; for I will magnify my name upon all those who receive and abide in my law" Doctrine & Covenants 132:63-65.

First, I find it curious that the laws of polygamy are only damning to the women who would stray, and speaks nothing of the men who do the same by courting women outside of their marriage. Furthermore, if he holds the Priesthood of the Mormon Church, his wife must abide by the church rules or be destroyed by God. Very strong words for a very unique set of beliefs.

The Mormon Church at the time received strong persecution from both political and religious leaders across the United States – and still holds a stigma today. The practice was considered illegal in many places in the U.S., and some church members were imprisoned for their involvement in the practice.

Mormons say that it was at this time that God 'realized' that his church was not going to be able to continue practicing polygamy at the risk of persecution, so in a revelation to Wilford Woodruff in 1890, God commanded that they stop practicing polygamy. On a side note, I would argue that God was omnipotent or all-knowing, and would not have designed a plan that would ultimately fail.

Never mind, Polygamy is Bad…

This command to cease the practice of polygamy was provided in the first Official Declaration ever made by the Mormon Church. Wilford Woodruff wrote, "Press dispatches having been sent for political purposes, from Salt Lake City, which have been widely published, to the effect that the Utah Commission, in their recent report to the Secretary of the Interior, allege that plural marriages are still being solemnized and that forty or more such marriages have been contracted in Utah since last June or during the past year, also that in public discourses the leaders of the Church have taught, encouraged and urged the continuance of the practice of polygamy— I, therefore, as President of the Church of Jesus Christ of Latter-day Saints, do hereby, in the most solemn manner, declare that these charges are false. We are not teaching polygamy or plural marriage, nor permitting any person to enter into its practice, and I deny that either forty or any other number of plural marriages have during that period been solemnized in our Temples or in any other place in the Territory. One case has been reported, in which the parties allege that the marriage was performed in the Endowment House, in Salt Lake City, in the Spring of 1889, but I have not been able to learn who performed the ceremony; whatever was done in this matter was without my knowledge. In consequence of this alleged occurrence the Endowment House was, by my instructions, taken down without delay. Inasmuch as laws have been enacted by Congress forbidding plural marriages, which laws have been pronounced constitutional by the court of last resort, I hereby declare my intention to submit to those laws, and to use my influence with the members of the Church over which I preside to have them do likewise. There is nothing in my teachings to the Church or in those of my associates, during the time specified, which can be reasonably construed to inculcate or encourage polygamy; and when any Elder of the Church has used language which appeared to convey any such teaching, he has been promptly reproved. And I now publicly declare that my advice to the Latter-day Saints is to refrain from contracting any marriage forbidden by the law of the land."

Several people will still claim that the Mormon practice of polygamy is still alive in the Mormon Church today. I will say that in my experience within the Mormon Church, not only is the practice of polygamy considered unacceptable, it is strictly forbidden. There are no circumstances to my knowledge under which it is considered to be acceptable, and any members claiming to be of the Mormon faith practicing polygamy are not associated with the Church of Jesus Christ of Latter Day Saints.

In fact, people in the Mormon Church found practicing polygamy will be excommunicated. However, that is only the practice of polygamy here on earth. If you are married and sealed in the temple and your spouse dies, men are permitted to marry and be sealed to their new wife. In doing this, they do not become 'unsealed' to their past wife, so they actually can have multiple wives in heaven. So they don't physically practice polygamy on earth, but the U.S. Courts don't have jurisdiction over heaven...

It is my personal belief that the LDS church did not stop performing plural marriages sincerely, simply because they changed their view on these types of marriages. These verses are still in their scriptures, and at any time the Prophet of the LDS Church could choose to revert back to these original beliefs of the church. I believe that they changed their opinion because modern culture found this belief to be unacceptable and they were fearful of persecution.

The best example of this is from an address of Wilford Woodruff later, regarding his manifesto. "The question is this: Which is the wisest course for the Latter-day Saints to pursue—to continue to attempt to practice plural marriage, with the laws of the nation against it and the opposition of sixty millions of people, and at the cost of the confiscation and loss of all the Temples, and the stopping of all the ordinances therein, both for the living and the dead, and the imprisonment of the First Presidency and Twelve and the heads of families in the Church, and the confiscation of personal property of the people (all of which of themselves would stop the practice); or, after doing and suffering what we have through our adherence to this principle to cease the practice and submit to the law, and through doing so leave the Prophets, Apostles and fathers at home, so that they can instruct the people and attend to the duties of the Church, and also leave the Temples in the hands of the Saints, so that they can attend to the ordinances of the Gospel, both for the living and the dead?" Doctrine & Covenants, Excerpts from three addresses by President Wilford Woodruff regarding the Manifesto.

To me, this address states it plainly that eradicating plural marriage was the lesser of two evils. Either they sacrifice the church to continue a practice which is written in their doctrine, or they sacrifice the controversial practice of polygamy. Rather than stick to the guns of their beliefs, they chose rather to adopt themselves to a new way of thinking.

In the 1998 general conference, Gordon Hinckley said, "I wish to state categorically that this Church has nothing whatever to do with those practicing polygamy. They are not members of this Church. Most of them have never been members…if any of our members are found to be practicing plural marriage, they are excommunicated; the most serious penalty the Church can impose. Not only are those doing so involved in direct violation of the civil law, they are in violation of the law of this Church."

There are those like the Fundamental Church of Jesus Christ of Latter-Day Saints (or FLDS members for short) who are not associated at all with the LDS church. These people are actually in all likelihood closer to the original beliefs of the Mormon Church. They practice a 'fundamentalist' view of Mormonism, adhering to those beliefs that were original to the LDS Church in its early days. Of course, that is my personal opinion and the FLDS Church will have to be reserved for another book entirely.

While Mormons will now state adamantly that they do not believe in polygamy, this change in belief does not dismiss the curious questions raised by the history of their faith. First, the Book of Mormon said that plural marriage was abominable. Then, the Doctrine & Covenants advocated it as a commandment given to Abraham and reinstated the practice in the Mormon Church through Joseph Smith, as a means to populate the earth with Mormon believers.

Later still, the Mormon Church flips their beliefs again to eradicate polygamy entirely, in an effort to save their religion from persecution. How can a faith be permitted to flip-flop their beliefs based on the whims of society at the time? You cannot simply believe something because it is convenient to do so. I personally prefer to hold on to the Bible, which has been steadfast and unchanging over the course of centuries, and has never changed its content for the sake of society.

Moralism

For those familiar with a person of Mormon faith, their most recognizable characteristic may be their morality. Mormons do not smoke, drink, or curse and they perform vast amounts of community service.

As you well know, Mormons are firmly planted in their belief of works required to attain their salvation and exaltation, and for this reason many acts of morality are required.

Mormon Underwear

To answer your burning question – no, I never wore the 'Mormon underwear' but yes, my family members do. For many, the Mormon underwear clause has been a point of curiosity for ages. Why do you need it? Does it have magical powers?

First, most Mormons will not refer to these undergarments as 'underwear', but rather just call them garments. They consider these garments to be sacred, and more important than most people would think their underwear to be. This is a foreign concept for most churchgoers, to think that the church has jurisdiction over your underwear – but the Mormon Church maintains that these garments are not very different from sacred garments worn by most cultures. Mormons will wear their garments daily, as an expression of constant faith in God.

Second, garments are actually pretty darn comfortable. It is made of similar materials to most underwear, in versions of cotton, polyester and nylon. Garments are only available in white to the general public. They do, however, provide special colored garments that are only available to active-duty military personnel.

For both men and women, there is a top and bottom piece. The top would be equivalent to an undershirt, covering the shoulders and the waistline, while the bottom for both men and women is similar to thin and fitted boxer briefs. For you women out there, yep, this would be a weird change.

Garments are primarily worn to promote modesty. They are typically concealed by the wearer's clothing so they are not revealed at all. This is particularly difficult for women, as most scoop-neck shirts or tank-tops are not an option of attire. This underwear is meant to replace any other underwear, so you are not supposed to wear it over any other type of undergarment. This holds true for women as well, who must wear their bras outside of their garments.

Of course, Mormons do not have to wear the garments when bathing, swimming, or having marital relations. It is at the discretion of the wearer when they should and should not wear it – but it is strongly advised that Mormons wear garments when possible. "And again, thou shalt not be proud in thy heart; let all thy garments be plain, and their beauty the beauty of the work of thine own hands; And let all things be done in cleanliness before me. Thou shalt not be idle; for he that is idle shall not eat the bread nor wear the garments of the laborer" Doctrine & Covenants 42:40-42.

Children are not required to wear garments. As part of their first visit to the temple, Mormons will receive their temple garments. This will be the first time they will wear their garments. From that point forward, it is their promise to God to wear it for the remainder of their life as a representation of their promises with God. Mormons will generally not discuss the ordinances which this symbolizes and keep those covenants secret from non-members.

They frequently point to Exodus 28:2-3 for their point of reference, where Moses made garments for Aaron "And thou shalt make holy garments for Aaron thy brother for glory and for beauty. And thou shalt speak unto all that are wise hearted, whom I have filled with the spirit of wisdom, that they may make Aaron's garments to consecrate him, that he may minister unto me in the priest's office." Basically, it is as a servant of God that people of the Mormon faith wear garments, to mirror Aaron's wearing of the garments as part of divine instruction.

As they feel that these ordinances are sacred, they also believe that the garments offer protective powers. While they do not protect them physically, they do offer the belief that garments offer them some sort of spiritual protection. The Mormon underwear or garments are really just symbolic representations of a covenant that Mormons make with God within the temple. Since they cannot express these covenants publically and they remain sacred in the temple, these may be a mystery that we cannot fully understand.

Chastity

Chastity is one of the most recognizable aspects in people of the Mormon faith. This is perhaps the Mormon Church's strongest convictions, and they hold their people strictly accountable for any actions that would speak against their Law of Chastity, which includes the every aspect of a relationship. Dating was a hard one for me.

In a day and age where people start dating when they get into middle school – and even more when they get into high school – having the Mormon Church dictate when I may date was extremely difficult. Mormon youth are not allowed to date until the age of sixteen, as dating is not viewed as getting to meet people, but rather strictly used for the purpose of finding a spouse. Even from the age of 16 it was impressed upon me that the only purpose in dating was to find a spouse, and until the age of 16, I was not prepared to handle that responsibility.

Upon early adulthood, the second important ideal to marriage is purity. This, of course, is not unlike most mainstream Christianity which also teaches the importance of abstinence and waiting until marriage. It is imperative within the Mormon faith that you remain pure until you are married in the Mormon temple to your spouse. They discourage any interactions between males and females that may place you into a situation where you could commit such a sin.

Self-control is also emphasized. They do not condone impulsive behavior, and discourage impure thoughts that lead to impure actions. Along these same lines, pornography is strictly prohibited. This includes any form of media that may create impure thoughts or emotions, as they are all equally sinful.

I'm not going to sit here and tell you that mainstream Christians promote pornography and impure actions. Of course they don't! But mainstream Christianity is also not hinging your entire salvation on your actions either. Again, we do good deeds and behave in a way that glorifies God – *not* to earn God's acceptance, but rather because we already have God's acceptance.

The Mormon Church even goes so far as to dictate the parameters of dating. They encourage only positive activities during dating, to distract from sexual tensions. They discourage any discussions that may promote promiscuity, and even discourage what they call 'passionate kissing'. Of course, such things are permissible once you are married. However, they caution strongly against adultery – as most Christian churches will. They instruct people to never flirt in any way, or ever be alone with anyone of the opposite sex.

Being obedient to the Law of Chastity is extremely important to people of the Mormon faith. It is fundamental to their actions towards the rest of the world, and possibly one of the things they are most well-known for. This belief in chastity is Biblical, but the Mormon Church has a very strong hold on their people in this respect. In many ways, these laws and rules are excellent guidelines for living a pure life. On the other hand, you must be sure to not lose sight of grace and the meaning of grace. Actions do not dictate salvation.

Speech

When I was about seven years old, boys were still yucky. I could accept their general existence, but to my friends, it was not cool to hang out with boys. Our age group in the LDS church at that time was too large to have everyone in one class, so they split us into two classes. One Sunday morning they announced our new church class groups. In one class there were five girls and four boys, and the other there were seven boys and one girl – and I was the one girl. I was the one girl, all by myself in a class with all boys. The cruelty! The nerve!

Needless to say, I was greatly displeased with the selection and I announced, "This is crap!" to my teacher and the class. I may have been only seven, but I knew the scale of bad words. There were some words that were bad yet acceptable, the words like 'butt-head' or 'stinky-face' that you could call your brother and get in minimal trouble. Then there were the blacklist words – the words that you knew you couldn't say without getting immediately drug out by your parents and spanked, or maybe given a bar of soap to munch on.

Crap was right in the middle of acceptability and unacceptability, and I was so deeply in the throes of torment that it escaped my lips before I even think twice about where I was. The teacher stopped, looked at me, and said nothing. 'Crap', I thought to myself, not out loud this time. Now I was really in trouble. No sooner did I get out of class before I found myself saddled in between the bishop and my mother, being told how 'crap' was a horrible word and I should repent immediately.

If you have ever spent any time with a Mormon, you may have noticed their impeccable speech. It is my opinion that your speech is a representation of who you are and what you stand for. This is the primary reason why Mormons do not curse or use the Lord's name in vain. Mormons have a reputation for only speaking in a way that God would smile upon.

Frankly, it would be nice if all churches could exercise such influence over the speech of their congregation and literally spread the good word. While many would argue that the clean speech perpetrated by Mormons is a result of the LDS church's control over their people, these beliefs in clean speech are very much Biblically rooted.

In Ephesians 4:29-31 say, "Let no corrupt communication proceed out of your mouth, but that which is good to use of edifying, that it may minister grace unto the hearers. And grieve not the Holy Spirit of God, whereby ye are sealed unto the day of redemption. Let all bitterness, and wrath, and anger, and clamor, and evil speaking, be put away from you, with all malice." In a few words, we should speak as if we are always ministering to others, as our examples should bring people closer to God through us.

We are all examples of God's wondrous miracles. Just as baptism and confirmation within Christianity are the fruits of our relationship with God, our speech should also exemplify Him. This is clearly demonstrated in Luke 6:44-45, "For every tree is known by his own fruit. For of thorns men do not gather figs, nor of a bramble bush gather they grapes. A good man out of the good treasure of his heart bringeth forth that which is good; and an evil man out of the evil treasure of his heart bringeth forth that which is evil: for of the abundance of the heart his mouth speaketh." We are all known by our behaviors, habits and actions.

Good works done for the gladness of God are not typically performed by those who spew evil words from their mouths. A strong relationship with God leads to the fruit of good speech, and an ability to affect others through the wholesomeness of your words.

Few would argue that any Christian church is a proponent of the use of foul language. However, while using poor language may reflect ill upon you and is frowned upon, the use of poor language has never been burden enough to condemn anyone to hell. Aside from setting a religious example, the other reason why Mormons are adamantly opposed to the use of foul language and taking the Lord's name in vain is also rooted in works.

The reason I was encouraged to repent after using the word 'crap' is rooted back in the Doctrine & Covenants 63:61-64, "Wherefore, let all men beware how they take my name in their lips – for behold, verily I say, that many there be who are under this condemnation, who use the name of the Lord, and use it in vain, having not the authority. Wherefore, let the church repent of their sins, and I, the Lord, will own them; otherwise they shall be cut off. Remember that that which cometh from above is sacred, and must be spoken with care, and by constraint of the Spirit; and in this there is no condemnation, and ye receive the Spirit through prayer; wherefore, without this there remaineth condemnation."

Using fowl language or taking the Lord's name in vain without repentance is equivalent to condemnation in the eyes of God. Repentance for every poor choice of words is yet another work required to receive God's grace within Mormonism.

Alcohol, Tobacco & Caffeine

Here's the hard one: consumption of alcohol and Christianity. This, similar to the Sacraments, is a grey area in which many denominations of Christianity do not agree. As it has been before, it will again be my goal not to be absolute on this issue, but rather simply state what the Bible says about the subject.

I believe that all mainstream Christian Churches, whether they believe in the consumption of alcohol or not, will agree that excessive consumption of alcohol is wrong. This belief is certainly Biblically sound. In Proverbs 20:1, "Wine is a mocker, strong drink is raging: and whosoever is deceived thereby is not wise." This Biblical reference is speaking against consumption of alcohol to the point of drunkenness, as the behavior of men is greatly influenced by its use.

Again in Proverbs 21:17 it says, "He that loveth pleasure shall be a poor man: he that loveth wine and oil shall not be rich." This verse warns not just against excessive drinking, but also against the gluttony of man; love of pleasure and fine things. A commonality between all of these verses is a condemnation of drinking alcohol *in excess*.

If that is a Biblical perspective of excessive drinking, then what is the view of drinking in the Mormon faith? Throughout our study of the Mormon faith, it has become apparent that when there is grey area of any kind in the Bible, Mormons will seek to fill it with their own scripture. In Doctrine & Covenants 89:5-9, Mormons believe that through revelation they were told not to partake of wine or hot beverages, which at the time included teas and coffees.

"That inasmuch as any man drinketh wine or strong drink among you, behold it is not good, neither meet in the sight of your Father, only in assembling yourselves together to offer up your sacraments before him. And behold, this should be wine, yea, pure wine of the grape of the vine, of your own make. And again, strong drinks are not for the belly, but for the washing of your bodies. And again, tobacco is not for the body, neither for the belly, and is not good for man, but is an herb for bruises and all sick cattle, to be used with judgment and skill. And again, hot drinks are not for the body or belly" Doctrine & Covenants 89:5-9.

These verses are the basis for the Mormon's argument against consuming caffeinated or hot beverages, alcohol or tobacco. I was sixteen before I ever tried my first cup of coffee and seventeen before I ever tried my first cup of iced tea. Throughout my childhood I knew it was a big no-no to consume beverages with caffeine in them including coffee and tea, tobacco, beer, wine or any alcoholic beverage whatsoever. I do remember my parents letting me drink those flavored sodas – orange, grape, strawberry, etc. – but none with caffeine in them. I attribute my bad dental visits as a child to those flavored sodas. Most of my family members to this day will not touch coffee, tea or alcohol in any form.

Tobacco is also strictly forbidden. Teas which possess caffeine are also forbidden, but non-caffeinated herbal teas are permitted. Generally speaking, all caffeinated beverages are frowned upon. This is because caffeine is viewed in the Mormon Church to be an addictive stimulant, and any product that is addictive in nature should be avoided.

One of the greatest controversies between the Mormons and the general public is probably the great Coca-Cola debate. So the burning question is: Does the Mormon Church own the Coca-Cola Company? Or just own significant stock in the Coca-Cola Company? Answer: these are both false. First, the Coca Cola Company is a multi-billion dollar conglomerate.

Owning just a 1% share in a company this size would cost roughly $1.4 billion. It would be impossible for the Mormon Church to own Coca-Cola outright, and Coca-Cola is far too large for any group to even own a noticeable fraction.

It has also been rumored that the Mormon Church owns stock in the Pepsi-Cola Company, and this is also false. Just as with Coca-Cola, Pepsi-Cola is also a multi-billion dollar conglomerate and any legitimate stock ownership would be prohibitively expensive.

So the next great question – Can Mormons drink sodas? The answer to this question is yes and no. The Mormon doctrine does speak against coffee, tea, tobacco and alcoholic beverages. It is interesting to note that the Mormon perspective on the 'hot beverage' commandment in their doctrine has largely disappeared. The focus on drinking hot beverages was most likely originally directed towards drinking coffee and hot teas, which do contain caffeine, but there is no specific directive against caffeine itself.

Mormons can and do drink hot beverages, such as hot chocolate and herbal teas which possess little to no caffeine. It would seem that the 'hot beverage' stipulation in their rule book has largely been refocused on caffeine, and they no longer take this the hot-beverage rule written in their own doctrine literally. But I suppose this is like many of the rules that they choose to tweak and no longer take literally, and they have decided to review this rule and tell themselves 'what it really means' now.

Once again, the Mormon view on their doctrine is open to interpretation. Many Church Presidents have spoken openly against drinking caffeine, as they view it to be a habit-forming drug. While the Mormon Doctrine does not specifically say that it is forbidden, Mormons will argue that heroin and cocaine are not mentioned in the Mormon Doctrine either but are viewed to be equally as evil.

In my opinion, this is a prime example of the Mormon Doctrine providing additions to the teachings of the Bible. Nowhere in the Bible are hot beverages or alcohol specifically banned from consumption. In fact, wine appears regularly throughout the Bible, and Jesus Himself drank it.

However, Mormons carry their own doctrine stating that they are banned. Of course, it is good practice to keep away from addictive substances and gluttonous behavior, and I would never deny that truth. But is it an actual commandment from God specifically not to drink alcohol, hot beverages or caffeine? Biblically speaking, the answer is no.

If the Bible specifically states that you cannot add to or take away from the Word, then it cannot be done. Since that is categorically what the Mormons have done through their doctrine, I must argue that this doctrine is untrue, unfounded, and without Biblical roots.

To all of these arguments, I would leave you with one Biblical reference from Romans. Romans 14:1 states, "Him that is weak in the faith receive ye, but not to doubtful disputations. For one believeth that he may eat all things: another, who is weak, eateth herbs. Let not him that eateth despise him that eateth not; and let not him which eateth not judge him that eateth: for God hath received him. Who are thou that judges another man's servant? To his own master he standeth or falleth. Yea, he shall be holden up: for God is able to make him stand…For none of us liveth to himself and no man dieth to himself. For whether we live, we live unto the Lord; and whether we die, we die unto the Lord: whether we live therefore, or die, we are the Lord's. For to this end Christ both died, and rose, and revived, that he might be Lord both of the dead and living. But why dost thou judge thy brother? Or why dost thou set at nought thy brother? For we shall all stand before the judgment seat of Christ…Let us not therefore judge one another anymore: but judge this rather, that no man put a stumbling block or an occasion to fall in his brother's way."

Rather than standing in judgment of one another for the actions that we believe to be correct according to the sails of our own conscience, we should leave the job to Christ. Instead, we should be spending that time in efforts to remove stumbling blocks from our neighbor's paths.

Tattoos, Piercings & Body Modifications

Tattoos are a difficult subject. In the Old Testament, Leviticus 19:28, there is a commandment given not to get in piercings or tattoos, saying "Ye shall not make any cuttings in your flesh for the dead, nor print any marks upon you: I am the Lord." However, in the New Testament we are no longer subject to the laws established in the Old Testament.

This is stated clearly in Galatians 3:23-25, "But before faith came, we were kept under the law, shut up unto the faith which should afterwards be revealed. Wherefore the law was our schoolmaster to bring us unto Christ, that we might be justified by faith. But after that faith is come, we are no longer under a schoolmaster."

The New Testament does not provide any specific laws related to body modifications. The New Testament abandonment of Old Testament law would suggest that Leviticus 19:28 is a law that no longer applies to Christians, and therefore body modifications are acceptable. However, many churches are opposed to tattoos and pierces because they feel they are a violation of 1 Corinthians 6:19-20.

1 Corinthians 6:19-20 states, "What? Know ye not that your body is a temple of the Holy Ghost which is in you, which ye have of God, and ye are not your own? For ye are bought with a price: therefore glorify God in your body, and in your spirit, which are God's." Your body and spirit were bought at a very high price, and should not be defiled. I would argue that so long as you are glorifying God with your choices and are making choices knowing that you are accountable to Him for those actions, then you take that upon yourself.

Mormons site a different verse when handling this difficult question. In 1 Corinthians 3:16-17, it states, "Know ye not that ye are the temple of God, and that the Spirit of God dwelleth in you? If any man defile the temple of God, him shall God destroy; for the temple of God is holy, which temple ye are." From a young age I was taught that my body was a temple, and it was my duty to keep that temple pure for God.

That included being free from tattoos and piercings – earrings being excluded, those seemed to be acceptable. Mormon leaders maintain that getting tattoos in any form is a show of disrespect for your body and therefore disrespect for God. More literally, they believe this to be another act of purity required to gain entry into the highest kingdom of heaven.

BLACKS IN THE CHURCH

The Black community has had a long history with the Mormon Church. For many years and still today, many people believe that the LDS Church is a 'whites only' organization. Mormons will maintain that this is untrue.

Congratulations! You're kind-of Members!

However, the Book of Mormon still contains a very powerful verse regarding why people possess the skin color they do. In the Book of Mormon, the Nephites had built a temple and were keeping to God's word, while the Lamanites had separated themselves. As a result of their disbelief in God, they received skin of blackness. This is shown in 2 Nephi 5:20-21, ". . . Inasmuch as they will not harken unto thy words they shall be cut off from the presence of the Lord. And behold, they were cut off from his presence. And he had caused the cursing to come upon them, yea, even a sore cursing, because of their iniquity. For behold, they had hardened their hearts against him, that they had become like unto a flint; wherefore, as they were white, and exceedingly fair and delightsome, that they might not be enticing unto my people the Lord God did cause a skin of blackness to come upon them."

Mormons claim that they have always been a fair organization that was kind and openly invited black people into their worship. If that was the case, then it is interesting to note that it was not until 1978 that the first black man was permitted to receive the priesthood. Prior to being allowed to receive the priesthood there have been black members of the church, some of whom were baptized in the church and were even pioneers who helped establish the church (although the 1860 census stated it was only 59 black people).

Despite not allowing black men to hold the priesthood until only thirty-two years ago, the Mormon Church had always maintained a strong opposition to slavery. While the Mormon Church still has a relatively small following amongst blacks, they do claim to be steadily growing these numbers in the United States and worldwide.

When slave-holders requested to join the Mormon Church, they were told that their slaves may come with them if they choose to, but if they do not wish to keep them they may sell them or let them go free – as their conscience dictates. They did not specify instructions, as the laws of the land still permitted slavery, but they did vocally discourage it. Furthermore, when the Nauvoo Temple was built, they allowed people of every race to be inside.

Just Kidding, You can Really Join Now

The concept of prophecy relates to all matters in the church, and the ability for blacks to receive the priesthood is no different.

In the second official declaration made by the Mormon Church, President Spencer W. Kimball wrote, "Aware of the promises made by the prophets and presidents of the Church who have preceded us that at some time, in God's eternal plan, all of our brethren who are worthy may receive the priesthood, and witnessing the faithfulness of those from whom the priesthood has been withheld, we have pleaded long and earnestly in behalf of these, our faithful brethren, spending many hours in the Upper Room of the Temple supplicating the Lord for divine guidance. He has heard our prayers, and by revelation has confirmed that the long-promised day has come when every faithful, worthy man in the Church may receive the holy priesthood, with power to exercise its divine authority, and enjoy with his loved ones every blessing that flows therefrom, including the blessings of the temple. Accordingly, all worthy male members of the Church may be ordained to the priesthood without regard for race or color. Priesthood leaders are instructed to follow the policy of carefully interviewing all candidates for ordination to either the Aaronic or the Melchizedek Priesthood to insure that they meet the established standards for worthiness."

Mormons cannot offer a reason why black Mormons were not allowed to receive the priesthood prior to 1978, although I would argue that the Book of Mormon states this quite clearly. They do maintain that while God did not specifically ban blacks from holding the priesthood, God allowed the ban to continue until he instructed the prophet (through revelation) to remove the ban.

Further to this, it has been suggested by LDS members that the reason why God did not reveal this to the prophet sooner was because of the scrutiny the Mormon Church would have received from pro-slavery groups. Again, it was an effort by the church to stay in line with the majority of the public, as to not be persecuted. It was a revelation given to Spencer W. Kimball in 1978 that changed this mindset.

Mormons are apologetic for their past stance of not permitting black men to receive the priesthood. They have said that all of the past should be forgotten in the light of what is now the present revelation. In the year 2000, there were 85,000 black Mormons in West Africa, and today there are even more.

TRIAL BY CHURCH

As you may have gathered from this study of Mormonism thus far, the Mormon faith is incredibly organized. They are structured similar to any modern day government, complete with an integral system of checks and balances. It is this impeccable structure which has permitted such explosive growth in their numbers, both in the motherland of Utah and throughout the world.

The Government of the Church

In 1834, the first Mormon High Council meeting was held in Ohio. There were twenty four High Priests gathered together at Joseph Smith's home, for the purpose of organizing themselves. This High Council was appointed by revelation, and would be used to settle controversies that may arise, which would not be possible to settle by the church or the Bishop's council.

They would have twelve high priests, and one or three presidents as needed. In the end there were nine high priests, seventeen elders, four priests and thirteen members. They together voted that the High Council would not have the power to act without at a minimum of seven of the appointed High Priests or their successors present.

Those seven High Priests would have the acting power to appoint other High Priests they considered worthy of the position, if other counselors were absent. Should there be vacancy through death, transgression, or removal from office, the President(s) of the church would nominate a person and submit their name for vote by the High Priests.

The President of the LDS Church also serves on this council, appointed by revelation. The President will be assisted by two other members of the Presidency. In the event the other two members are absent, the President may act alone. If the President is absent, either of the other two Presidency members can act in his place.

The Quorum of the Twelve will each pick a number, determining which of them is to speak first at the meetings of the High Council. "Whenever this council convenes to act upon any case, the twelve councilors shall consider whether it is a difficult one or not; if it is not, two only of the counselors shall speak upon it, according to the form above written. But if it is through to be difficult, four shall be appointed; and if more difficult, six; but in no case shall more than six be appointed to speak" Doctrine & Covenants 102:13-14. Just as a trial in the United States courts, the person standing accused in front of the church has a right to council, in an effort to prevent an injustice from occurring.

Those who are selected to speak before the council present their case and any evidence they can provide. "Those counselors who draw even numbers, that is, 2, 4, 6, 8, 10 and 12, are the individuals who are to stand up in behalf of the accused, and prevent insult and injustice" Doctrine & Covenants 102:17. The accused person is permitted to speak for themselves once their counselors who were chosen to speak on their behalf have spoken.

After all evidence is submitted and reviewed, and all those involved have testified, the President will render a verdict and call upon the twelve counselors to provide their votes. If at any time one of the twelve counselors finds the President's decision to be in error, they can speak up to the council and a retrial will be commenced. The first verdict will stand unless new light is shone upon the case during the retrial.

On a side note, I find it fascinating that as the U.S. Court System was also in its infancy (just like our Constitution), the Mormon Church developed its own 'court' system nearly identical to the country's court system. For example, in felony cases the jury is made of twelve people – and the High Priest Council also has twelve people. In lesser criminal and civil cases the jury is made of six people – just as the High Priest Council which hears cases has six people. There was a very apparent mirroring of the U.S. Judicial system being established here.

At some points, there may not be the Mormon doctrine in existence to answer the question of whether or not the person in question is guilty. Just as Americans create laws when laws are absent but necessary, the Mormon

Church can also create laws as necessary. "In the case of difficulty respecting the doctrine of principle, if there is not sufficiency written to make the case clear to the minds of the council, the President may inquire and obtain the mind of the Lord by revelation" Doctrine & Covenants 102:23.

Since there are many churches throughout the world promoting the Mormon beliefs, the High Priests are allowed to call and organize a council while they are on the road, as necessary. "It shall be the duty of said council to transmit, immediately, a copy of their proceedings, with a full statement of the testimony accompanying their decision, to the high council of the seat of the First Presidency of the Church" Doctrine & Covenants 102:26. Should anyone be unhappy with the verdict rendered by that council, they can file an appeal with the First Presidency of the Church to have a retrial.

These High Priest councils are only required in very complicated church issues, considered to be too difficult or widespread for the smaller churches to handle. High Priests that travel abroad may discern whether or not this type of a council is necessary for a case.

However, you can appeal decisions made by the High Council or traveling High Priests, but you cannot appeal decisions made by the Quorum of the Twelve Apostles. The only time it is deemed acceptable to question the decisions made by the Quorum of the Twelve is when the issue of transgression may arise.

The law of the Mormon Church is considered to be the ultimate authority in their faith. "And the Presidency of the council of the High Priesthood shall have power to call other high priests, even twelve, to assist as counselors; and thus the Presidency of the High Priesthood and its counselors shall have power to decide upon testimony according to the laws of the church. And after this decision it shall be had in remembrance no more before the Lord; for this is the highest council of the church of God, and a final decision upon controversies in spiritual matters. There is not any person belonging to the church who is exempt from this council of the church" Doctrine & Covenants 107:79-81.

The authority of the church in spiritual matters is final. Likewise, if a President of the High Priesthood were to sin against his position, a decision would be rendered against him by the common council of the church.

Oh Man, you are in TROUBLE

So what are those sins which are worthy of discussion in front of your church elders, you may ask? Within the Doctrine and Covenants, there are several examples of trial-worthy issues, the main issue being adultery. "Behold, verily I say unto you, that whatever persons among you, having put away their companions for the cause of fornication, or in other words, if they shall testify you in all lowliness of heart that this is the case, ye shall not cast them out from among you; But if ye shall find that any persons have left their companions for the sake of adultery, and they themselves are the offenders, and their companions are living, they shall be cast out from among you" Doctrine & Covenants 42:74-75.

For lack of a better term, Mormons believe in shunning members of their society who they believe have sinned against the principles of God. It would seem that at this lowly point in a person's life, they would benefit most from being surrounded by people who wish to help them, not outcast from their society and made to live in loneliness. But I suppose that rules are rules.

1. *Adultery:* "And if any man or woman shall commit adultery, he or she shall be tried before two elders of the church, or more, and every word shall be established against him or her by two witnesses of the church, and not of the enemy; but if there are more than two witnesses it is better. But he or she shall be condemned by the mouth of the two witnesses; and the elders shall lay the case before the church, and the church shall lift up their hands against him or her, that they may be dealt with according to the law of God." Doctrine & Covenants 42:80-82.

2. *Murder:* " And it shall come to pass, that if any persons among you shall kill they shall be delivered up and dealt with according to the laws of the land; for remember that he hath no forgiveness; and it shall be proved according to the laws of the land" Doctrine & Covenants 42:79.

You may recall that in Mormonism, murder is considered to be an unforgiveable sin, which will prevent a person from gaining their salvation. Those people are subject to the laws of the land and gain no forgiveness from the church.

Permission to Nark

I was born in Utah, and while I do not remember living there because I was too young, my parents told me fascinating stories of the people there. Particularly in Utah, there is quite a bit of tattling that goes on. My mother told me (and other Mormons have collaborated) that other members of the church would dig through her garbage when she put it out at night, to see if they had thrown away any beer bottles or other incriminating materials that could be brought before the church.

"And if thy brother or sister offend thee, thou shalt take him or her between him or her and thee alone; and if he or she confess thou shalt be reconciled. And if he or she confess not thou shalt delivery him or her up unto the church, not to the members, but to the elders. And it shall be done in a meeting, and that not before the world. And if thy brother or sister offend many, he or she shall be chastened before many. And if any one offend openly, he or she shall be rebuked openly, that he or she may be ashamed. And if he or she confess not, he or she shall be delivered up unto the law of God" Doctrine & Covenants 42:88-91.

It is both silly and sad that people must live in constant fear and judgment of one another. To me, the New Testament of the Bible really tells a story of forgiveness, love and acceptance. These rules and regulations seem to oppose those principles, seeking to unveil the worst faults in people rather than celebrate the good.

The Mormon lifestyle is truly a lifestyle, with a set of rules, regulations and penalties all its own. The law of God runs parallel in people's lives with the law of the land, and people hold each other responsible for their actions. It is truly a Utopian ideal, each person accountable to the other for the greater good of the whole. It seems, though, that by creating your own court of God, the Mormon faith is actually permitting people to play God.

To reference Matthew 7:1-2 again, "Judge not, that ye be not judged. For with what judgment ye judge, ye shall be judged: and with what measure ye mete, it shall be measured to you again." The Bible makes it clear that only God will be the judge and jury on the final judgment day. Though we may do things that are not Christ-like, it is not our duty to stand in judgment or tattle on one another. God is omnipotent, and he sees all things. Rather than creating a court of God, it would seem more in line with Christianity to believe that he already knows.

TITHING & FINANCES

The Mormon Church is one of the wealthiest churches in the United States, and perhaps even the world. The Mormon Church does not disclose their worth, even to members of the faith. In fact, there are probably only a handful of people who know the details of the church's total wealth.

Based on their assets, business dealings and stocks, several estimates have been made that the Mormon Church has an overall worth in the neighborhood of $30 billion.

It is mandatory within the Mormon Church to pay ten percent of your income to the church. Doctrine & Covenants 119:3-5, "And this shall be the beginning of the tithing of my people…those who have thus been tithed shall pay one-tenth of their interest annually; and this shall be a standing law unto them forever, for my holy priesthood, saith the Lord. Verily I say unto you, it shall come to pass that all those who gather unto the land of Zion shall be tithed of their surplus properties, and shall observe this law, or they shall not be found worthy to abide among you."

Paying this tithe qualifies members to enter into their temples. Failure to do so means being disqualification from temple entrance, and therefore inability to perform the sacred ordinances required to enter into the Celestial kingdom of heaven. It has been said by LDS leaders that a man who does not have enough faith to pay his tithes, does not have enough faith to save his family (through baptisms for the dead). This is a stiff price to literally pay to enter the kingdom of God.

Now, please do not misinterpret my views on the responsibility of tithing. The principle of tithing dates back to the Old Testament, and is mentioned in several books in the Bible, such as Genesis and Leviticus.

One of the most popular references to tithes comes in Malachi 3:10, "Bring ye all the tithes into the storehouse, that there may be meat in mine house, and prove me now herewith, saith the Lord of hosts, if I will not open you the windows of heaven, and pour you out a blessing, that there shall not be room enough to receive it."

The New Testament does not make mention of tithes nearly as much as the Old Testament, but that is not to say that giving graciously to the church is unimportant.

As we said before, there are many fruits of a relationship with God. One of those fruits is giving to others and giving to the Church. All things belong to God, and it is our responsibility to provide for the church, which provides for each of us in its own way. "Now therefore, our God, we thank thee, and praise thy glorious name. But who am I, and what is my people, that we should be able to offer so willingly after this sort? For all things come of thee, and of thine own have we given thee" 1 Chronicles 29:13-14.

By providing for our churches, we are able to help the church to grow and touch more lives, bringing more people in to faith through Christ. Tithes or donations to the church should be given gladly and with a good heart, not begrudgingly and forced by church mandate.

For Mormons, tithing is also considered to be an exercise of control. In knowing that ten percent of their income will go to the church, people exercise more control over their finances. In fact, the Mormon Church exercises quite a bit of control over the people of their faith in terms of finances. "Behold, it is said in my laws, or forbidden, to get in debt to thine enemies" Doctrine & Covenants 64:27.

Again, it is said in Doctrine & Covenants 104:78, "And again, verily I say unto you, concerning your debts – behold it is my will that you shall pay all your debts." Not only is debt greatly discouraged, but it is also considered imperative to your salvation to always be paid up on your tithes.

There is a treasury where all the finances of the Mormon Church are kept, as was also commanded in the Doctrine & Covenants chapter 104. One person is appointed to run the treasury, which belongs to no one person in the church, but rather belongs to the church itself. The funds for the church are to be used for those things which promote the church, such as printing the Mormon scriptures and building new churches and temples.

There is then a second treasury with its own appointed person running it. All money generated by stocks, properties, or other such money making assets are all placed in this second treasury. The council makes decisions regarding when these finances are spent, and on what or to whom they can be given.

My grandparents and many of my family members have diligently given their tithes and additional monies to the LDS church, believing that in providing these things to the church, they are sealing themselves a place in the highest level of heaven. While it is most definitely good to provide for the church and promote the growth of our faith, it is important to be able to distinguish between works and grace. By the very definition of grace, we are saved by our faith and not our tithes. Bottom line is, tithing is good, it is Biblically sound, but you cannot buy your entry ticket into heaven.

BEING PREPARED, PROVIDING FOR THE POOR

The LDS church has always operated on the 'teach a man to fish' mentality, believing that it is always better to provide people with skills rather than just give people handouts. During natural disasters, the Mormon Church is able to dispatch food, materials and finances globally within just hours. Their focus is to ensure that the long-term requirements of the community are fulfilled, rather than providing short-term solutions.

The Mormon Church's goal is to provide people with skills to sustaining themselves, enabling them to become reliant only upon themselves, for "if ye are prepared, ye shall not fear" Doctrine & Covenants 38:30. Some such training includes neonatal resuscitation training, clean water projects, wheelchair distribution, and visual treatment and disease vaccinations.

Calling the Hotline

The Mormon Church has a huge financial network. Emergency disaster relief finances are often donated from members of the church, and one percent of all tithes reside in their humanitarian aid fund. All of this funding is provided directly to the area in need, and the Mormon Church typically absorbs their overhead costs to accomplish this. However, most of the preparedness from church members is actually focused on the individual members and families of the church.

Since I can remember and even still today, my family has kept a stash of food under the stairs. Wheat, flour, rice and other grains were stashed in large barrels, tucked underneath the stairs and available in the event of a disaster. When we were little and a tornado warning would come on the news, my parents would have us lay in sleeping bags underneath the stairs, next to the buckets.

The Mormon Church encourages all church members to carry a one year's supply of bare necessities in their homes. In the event of flood, famine, earthquake, hurricane or other natural disasters, the ultimate goal is to always be prepared. They also encourage people to grow their own food and eat from their own farm of crops, even grow food on your balcony of your apartment if you have no yard. The Mormon Church encourages saving money and resources, in preparation for the day when it may become necessary to utilize those skills and resources.

Build Thee a Storehouse

As many mainstream Christian churches do, Mormons encourage the giving to those less fortunate. "And behold, thou wilt remember the poor, and consecrate of thy properties for their support that which thou hast to impart unto them, with a covenant and a deed which cannot be broken" Doctrine & Covenants 42:30.

They are also encouraged to only keep that which is necessary to their own existence, and give the rest to others. This led to the creation of what is called a Storehouse. In the early church, a Storehouse was created to collect grains and commodities for the needy people of the church. Today there are 146 Storehouses that serve people throughout the Western Hemisphere. These Storehouses are typically stocked by donations made to the church, and run on a volunteer basis.

"Therefore, the residue shall be kept in my storehouse, to administer to the poor and the needy, as shall be appointed by the high council of the church, and the bishop and his council" Doctrine & Covenants 42:34.

However, the items in the Storehouses are not simply given to church members. The church members are given the opportunity to work in a capacity where they are capable, in exchange for the items that they receive. These beliefs are best illustrated in Doctrine & Covenants 56: 16-18, "Wo unto you rich men, that will not give your substance to the poor, for your riches will canker your souls; and this shall be your lamentation in the day of visitation, and of judgment, and of indignation: The harvest is past, the summer is ended, and my soul is not saved! Wo unto you poor men, whose hearts are not broken, whose spirits are not contrite, and whose bellies are not satisfied, and whose hands are not stayed from laying hold upon other men's goods, whose eyes are full of greediness, and who will not labor with your own hands! But blessed are the poor who are pure in heart, whose hearts are broken, and whose spirits are contrite, for they shall see the kingdom of God coming in power and great glory unto their deliverance; for the fatness of the earth shall be theirs." Those who are rich must give to the poor, and those who are poor must earn their keep. In this Utopian society, all members are contributors as required by God.

There are also specific laws written in the Doctrine & Covenants regarding women and children that are without husbands and fathers, and how they should be taken care of by the church. According to the laws of the church shown in Doctrine & Covenants 83, women have their husbands to 'maintain' them. However, when their husbands die, they can rely on the church to support them so long as they are faithful to the church.

Children should also rely on their parents for maintenance until they are old enough to maintain themselves. Those children without parents can rely upon the church storehouses for support, if their parents left them no inheritance. "And the storehouses shall be kept by the consecrations of the church; and widows and orphans shall be provided for, as also the poor. Amen" Doctrine & Covenants 83:6.

Is taking care of others a good idea? Absolutely. No one can fault the LDS church for doing an excellent job at helping those in greatest need. In my opinion, more people should have the level of consideration and love for others both in and out of their churches that the Mormon Church does.

However, these requirements are not mandated in the Bible for the purpose of salvation. I would emphasize to you that there is a very distinguishable difference between good works that are commendable and good in the eyes of God, and good works gaining you access to heaven. Mormons do these good works because they are commanded to in the Mormon scriptures, for the ultimate purpose of gaining salvation.

Nowhere in the Bible are there these specific instructions given with regards to how to tend to the poor and the creation of storehouses. Many people will stand back and look at the Mormons, marveling at how they care for each other and the needy.

People view their actions and think that they must be part of a unique society of individuals that know something the mainstream Christians don't – after all, how can they be so good? Preparedness and caring for the needy are all benevolent actions.

The question we must ask is not whether or not these works are good, but whether or not these works are required to gain access to heaven. The Mormon doctrine says they are, and the Bible does not. These specific instructions are undoubtedly another addition to the teachings of the Bible, as they create a clear outline of actions and requirements that the Bible does not illustrate.

Mormon Temples

The Mormon temples are among the most beautiful buildings in the world. They are considered to be the literal houses of God, where they provide ordinances needed for Mormon to attain their salvation and exaltation.

Endowment Ceremonies

One of the ordinances that can be received in the temple is what Mormons call their endowment. This word means 'gift'. Mormons believe that their endowment is a gift from God. It is a series of instructions Mormons believed to be provided by God, and covenants required to adhere to the Mormon gospel. These instructions are centered on God and Jesus (again, viewed in the Mormon faith as two separate individuals), and Jesus' role in God's plan.

The Endowment must be received before people can participate in a mission or be married in the Mormon temple. The individual receiving the endowment will actually go through the ceremony twice. First they will go through the ceremony on their own behalf. Then they will go through the entire ceremony again on behalf of a deceased person of their same gender.

The person receiving the Endowment will go into the temple and change into their temple undergarments, and then put on a white sheet-type covering. They will then receive a washing and anointing ritual performed by temple members of the same gender.

"Then the white stone mentioned in Revelation 2:17, will become a Urim and Thummim to the individual who receives one, whereby things pertaining to a higher order of kingdoms will be made known; and a white stone is given to each of those who come into the celestial kingdom, whereon is a new name written, which no man knoweth save he that receiveth it. The new name is the key word." This name given is a new and secret name that you will be given for eternity. It can be something like Mark or James for men, or Stephanie or Sarah for girls. It is forbidden to ever reveal this secret temple name to anyone for any reason.

The individual then changes into a white dress or shirt and pants over their garments, and carries a bag with a materials including a green apron, a white robe and a cap or veil to be worn later in the Endowment ceremony. They then go into an auditorium with several other people, men sitting on one side and women sitting on the other.

They watch a video showing the creation of the world and the fall of Adam. Then Peter, James and John are shown, instructing the individuals on handshakes and passwords that will be necessary to gain entry into the Celestial Kingdom of heaven. They will then role play to solidify and practice this new knowledge, one person playing the part of God and the others trying to gain entry into heaven.

They have then received their Endowment, or gift of knowledge pertaining to the highest level of heaven. Once they receive their endowment, they also receive their garments. They are obligated to wear these garments as they have been instructed in their endowment. These garments are a reminder of covenants made in the temple, and are viewed as a protection against temptation and evil.

On a side note, I find it very interesting that the Apostles of the New Testament of the Bible are 'in' on the secret handshakes and passwords of heaven. If there were special entrance requirements into heaven, why did the Apostles not disclose those in the New Testament? And if there were three levels of heaven with super special entry requirements to get into the highest level, why would the Celestial kingdom as one of three levels of heaven never be mentioned at all in the Bible?

Mormons will rarely if ever speak about their temple ceremonies. Up until the early 1990's when they changed the ceremonial oaths, Mormons swore upon their lives not to speak of the covenants they took in the Mormon temple. For this reason, there is little documented and spoken about the actual temple rituals, and these rituals remain secret to most of us.

Celestial Marriages

A second and very important ordinance is called celestial marriage. Through this ordinance and only in temples, husbands and wives are sealed to each other for 'time and all eternity'. This is where you may see the 'Families Can Be Together Forever' concept displayed in Mormon homes and songs. So long as both the husbands and wives are faithful to the covenants they made in the temple, they will be sealed together in heaven as they are sealed together on earth.

If a husband and wife are sealed in the temple and then have children, their children are also born in the covenant. Those children born in the covenant are automatically sealed to their parents and are part of an eternal family. Children who are not born into the covenant can later become part of the covenant once their parents become sealed to one another.

Baptisms for the Dead

As you already know, the fourth ordinance performed in temples is baptism for the dead. Mormons believe that those who have died and are not Mormons will have the opportunity to select to accept this doctrine in the spirit world before the second coming of Jesus. Mormons will act on behalf of their deceased ancestors by being baptized, confirmed, receive endowments, and participate in sealing husbands, wives and families together in their names.

Again on a side note, I really still don't understand how the whole 'making a decision in heaven' thing works. If you are in heaven, wouldn't you see that there are three levels of heaven? And wouldn't that tell you automatically that the Mormon Church was right? It does not seem logical to me that you would have a decision once you landed in the spirit world because it seems like the truth would be obvious. Why would you not convert to Mormonism in the spirit world if the apparent alternative was damnation? Seems like an easy decision to me.

Temple-Worthiness

All of these ordinances are performed inside of Temples, which are generally not open to the public. Mormons who visit the temples must be considered 'temple worthy', meaning that they have kept all commandments, are in good standing with the Mormon Church, and are spiritually prepared to perform the works in the temple. To become temple worthy, Mormon members must have two interviews.

First, they must meet with a member of the Bishopric or a Branch President. Then they will meet with a member of the Stake Presidency or a Mission President. In these interviews, church members will be asked about their personal conduct, and whether or not they are worthy to enter the temple. Church members will also certify that they are worthy to enter the Mormon temple. Having the authority of these people to enter the temple is called having your 'temple recommend'.

Just as Mormons must wear garments daily outside of the temple, there are also special clothing requirements inside the temple. Mormons are instructed to wear their best clothing to the temple. Once inside the temple, they exchange their clothing for white temple clothing.

They then have a locker and a private dressing space to change into their temple clothing. They believe that since they are all dressed similarly in white, all Mormons feel closeness with God and are all viewed as equal to each other, since they are all in the same attire.

Temples are also used as a place for revelations. Since it is a place of great spiritual integrity, it is a place where the church leaders can ask for spiritual guidance on pivotal issues. There are many secretive topics inside the temple which are not shared with the general public.

"Therefore, verily I say unto you, that your anointings, and your washings, and your baptisms for the dead, and you solemn assemblies, and your memorials for your sacrifices by the sons of Levi, and for your oracles in your most holy places wherein you receive conversations, and your statutes and judgments, for the beginning of the revelations and the foundation of Zion, and for the glory, honor and endowment of all her municipals, are ordained by the ordinance of my holy house, which my people are always commanded to build unto my holy name. And verily I say unto you, let this house be built unto my name, that I may reveal mine ordinances therein unto my people" Doctrine & Covenants 124:39-40.

Temples are built for very significant purposes in the Mormon Church. They are built to perform sacred works and ordinances that are the cornerstone of the Mormon faith. While Mormons may claim that endowments, celestial marriage, the sealing of families, baptisms for the dead, and performing numerous services by proxy are mandatory for salvation, I will again point to the Bible in the book of Ephesians, which says that we are all saved by grace through our faith, independent of our works.

It is not possible for these acts to be requirements for salvation, as the Bible specifically says that acts are not required. You cannot create ordinances in any scripture that are contrary or additional to the teachings of the Bible, and the Bible says so itself.

COMING TO TERMS WITH GRACE

Faith is confusing. For some, God is an influence in your life from the beginning. For others, we have to walk a long path before we can find ourselves in His grace. For me, God wasn't just opening up the Bible at Genesis and starting to read a story. It had nothing to do with what I believed, because I was so confused about what to believe at all.

It really came down to what I don't believe, and explaining Christianity in my mind, only backwards. Some days it seemed like I was Alice tumbling down the rabbit hole, grasping at things as I continued to fall. And then one day I hit the ground, everything started to make sense, and I had to ask myself some tough questions. Where did my original beliefs come from? What rules can't you just make up? How deep does the rabbit hole go?

You see, not all people have the gift of evangelism and most people don't know how to minister to people of other faiths, especially Mormons. Mormonism is a very dangerous religion. From the outside, they carry the image of Christianity and love of Christ. But as you can see throughout this book, every aspect of mainstream Christianity has been altered and adapted – somehow morphed into a completely different faith altogether.

I knew what baptism and sacrament and the Bible were, but they were words that had an entirely different meaning and depth in the Mormon faith. Figuring out Christianity wasn't just opening up a catechism and figuring out what the mainstream Christian religions believed.

It was opening up all of the question marks of faith in my heart and then figuring out what they meant, and whether or not I believed in everything I had ever been taught. Not just simply learning Christianity, but decompressing everything I had ever been told about God, unraveling it, straightening it all back out and digesting it again.

Mormons believe in the Bible. But they also believe that the Bible is an incomplete and errant Word of God, made more perfect through the addition of three other texts. My first stop on the way to Christianity was coming to the resolution that the Bible is the Word of God, and then knowing that I could therefore only turn to the Bible and the Bible alone for answers. Through writing this book and growing my own knowledge of God, I have come to understand a few important facts.

First, most points of contention made by Mormons are actually addressed in the Bible, and distorted through the other Mormon texts and interpretations. Second, I had to come to an understanding that there are some things that God intended to be beyond our human comprehension.

No matter how desperately we may want answers to those questions that burn inside of us, it is not the responsibility of man to create solutions to resolve those issues. Mormons will stand back and poke holes in mainstream Christianity, while simultaneously creating doctrine to fill those holes.

Then they can sit back and ask people to come to their faith, because they have all the answers. However, by filling those holes with new doctrine, they have completely changed the face of Christianity. There are many questionable beliefs touted by Mormons that are loosely based on the Bible, if Biblically based at all:

- Jesus visiting the Americas subsequent to his resurrection
- The creation of the Book of Mormon as a book inspired by God
- The creation of the Doctrine & Covenants as a book of rules and promises from God through revelations
- The creation of the Pearl of Great Price as a historical document of the Mormon Church
- A living prophet who can alter the Mormon doctrine and beliefs
- The Trinity does not exist, they are three separate individuals and not of one essence
- Grace does not exist, you are judged by works
- Original Sin does not exist, and man can be perfect
- Salvation is not by grace, but by works
- There are three levels of heaven based on those works

- Reinterpretation of Biblical passages based on revelations by man
- Establishment of Baptisms for the Dead
- Establishment of marriage sealing and children sealing, also available by proxy
- Creation of covenants and ordinances in endowment which must be followed to earn celestial glory
- Establishment and subsequent removal of the commandment of polygamy
- Secret passwords, handshakes and knowledge required to enter the highest level of heaven

If you are Mormon, you change the entire meaning of Christianity. How so? If you believe that Jesus came to America, then you believe there are texts aside from the Bible. If you believe in living Mormon Prophets today, then you believe that God's Word is incomplete and can be changed at any time, even if those changes add to or contradict the Bible.

If the Trinity does not exist and Jesus is just the literal son of God, then you believe that Jesus is lesser than God because he was created by God. If you do not believe in grace, then you do not believe in the principles under which Jesus died on the cross. Without grace, you believe that all people will be judged for their actions and salvation is made through works. If you believe in salvation through works, then you cannot believe in the words of the Bible, as Ephesians specifically states that we are not saved by our works. If you do not believe in original sin, then you believe that all people are inherently sinless and therefore being without sin is actually something we can attain. If we can be without sin, then we are saying that we can be equal to Jesus.

These are among the many questionable principles of Mormonism. These are major, major differences from mainstream Christianity. It is so important to look at these differences, and really recognize that you must take a few steps back from your own understanding of Christianity to witness to a Mormon.

Their Jesus is not truly your Jesus, though he may bear the same name. Your salvation is not their salvation, though you may use the same word to describe it. You really have to step back and ask yourself, why is Mormonism not considered to be just another denomination of Christianity, and why do major religious parties view Mormonism to be a cult?

I have a strong personal belief about the subject of Mormonism, after reading the doctrine and speeches of the church and having been a member myself for many years.

It is fascinating to me how contorted the Bible becomes once the Mormon doctrines are introduced. It is fascinating to me that the words of one man can create an empire of a religion, and that people will blindly follow a man who claims not only to have divine revelations, but to be the only person on earth who can do so. It is fascinating to me that Mormons can claim to believe in the Bible while at the same time both adding to it and using the Doctrine & Covenants to completely change the meanings of certain passages through revelation, despite the fact that Deuteronomy 4:2 says, "Ye shall not add unto the word which I command you, neither shall ye diminish ought from it, that ye may keep the commandments of the Lord your God which I command you."

It is my personal belief that the Mormon doctrine is inspired of angels, but not the angels of heaven. Frankly, it is too well written and unbelievably deceptive to be entirely made by the hand of man.

I would again say that Mormonism is foreseen in Galatians 1:6-9, "I marvel that ye are so soon removed from him that called you into the grace of Christ unto another gospel: which is not another; but there be some that trouble you, and would pervert the gospel of Christ. But through we, or an angel from heaven, preach any other gospel unto you than that which we have preached unto you, let him be accursed."

The Mormon Church has long paraded itself under the umbrella of Christianity, but you must understand that this is not a true Christian Church. The God worshipped and the principles practiced within this religion are completely baseless, not holding true to the principles of Christianity at all.

They have taken the foundation rooted in Christ and contorted grace into something that is not grace at all. It saddens me deeply to know that there are people who will follow this faith blindly, as it is one of the most deceptive distortions of God's Word that I have ever witnessed.

Perhaps the most profound quotation I have ever read related to Mormonism was that of Orson Pratt, a leader of the Mormon Church and an original member of the Quorum of the Twelve Apostles.

In his pamphlet entitled, *Devine Authenticity of the Book of Mormon* in 1851, he wrote, "If false, it is one of the most cunning, wicked, bold, deep-laid impositions ever palmed upon the world, calculated to deceive and ruin millions who will sincerely receive it as the word of God, and will suppose themselves securely built upon the rock of truth until they are plunged with their families into hopeless despair." I could not have said it better myself.

Mormonism is complicated. I didn't know what I didn't know. It took me a great amount of re-education before I could fully comprehend those concepts that many of my Christian friends found to be so incredibly fundamental. And while there are many Mormons who are devout in their faith, there are also many Mormons who hold great doubts in their hearts.

It is to these people that we all have responsibility to witness, and for those people that I hope you have opened your eyes and hearts to understand their distorted view of the Bible and Christ. We have been called to witness to those who may otherwise never know the real truth about Christ, and the wonderful gift of grace that he has so mercifully given to us. It is never too late to be a soldier for God.

www.ingramcontent.com/pod-product-compliance
Lightning Source LLC
Chambersburg PA
CBHW051057230426
43667CB00013B/2330